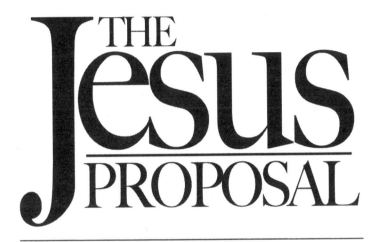

THE JESUS PROPOSAL

A THEOLOGICAL FRAMEWORK FOR MAINTAINING
THE UNITY OF THE BODY OF CHRIST

Rubel Shelly
& John O. York

LEAFWOOD
PUBLISHERS

THE JESUS PROPOSAL
Maintaining the Unity of the Body of Christ
published by Leafwood Publishers

Copyright © 2003 by Rubel Shelly & John O. York

ISBN 0-9748441-1-X
Printed in the United States of America

Cover design by Rick Gibson

For information:
Leafwood Publishers, Siloam Springs, AR
1-877-634-6004 (toll free)

Visit our website: www.leafwoodpublishers.com

04 05 06 07 08   9 8 7 6 5 4 3 2

Dedication

To

The Family of God at Woodmont Hills
for permitting us to

preach, exchange ideas about, and

participate in implementing

The Jesus Proposal

with your insights, encouragement, and grace.

You have taught us so much.

TABLE OF CONTENTS

PREFACE

The unity of the body of Christ is not a desirable option. It is a divine mandate. It is also a practical necessity for leading the world to believe in Jesus.

But the world has just passed through a 200-year period during which oneness among Christians has been practically impossible. It was not theology so much as culture which created that impossibility. Or, stated more precisely, the Enlightenment culture generated a divisive approach to theology that kept Christians apart.

Modernity, the name we have fixed to that culture, demanded fixed, rational, and clearly marked boundaries. It formulated categories for classification purposes. It labeled and assigned. It judged and excluded. It fostered and furthered division.

Now there has been a major paradigm shift to what is called—for the lack of a better term—Postmodernity. It acknowledges and embraces a degree of ambiguity that Modernity could not tolerate. It sees fuzzy rather than fixed boundaries. It resists rigid categories, judgmentalism, and exclusion; it affirms inclusion, association, and flexibility. In its extreme forms, Postmodernity is as dangerous for its "fuzziness" as Modernity was for its "rigidity."

The "proposal" of *The Jesus Proposal* is that Christians from all denominations can benefit from this cultural shift. In the Postmodern atmosphere of the twenty-first century, we can experience relational unity in Christ—unity greater and more important than theological agreement, ecclesiological structure, and institutional loyalty.

Jesus Christ should mean more than denomination or theological tradition or method of interpreting the Bible. We believe that the relational faith we are proposing has a better chance for acceptance now than ever in the past two centuries. And we believe it is closer to the experiences of the church one reads about in the New Testament than we have known.

We have enjoyed the stimulation of thinking, praying, and talking through these ideas. Now we welcome you to the process.

Rubel Shelly
John O. York

1. *God Is Not Far From Us*

Rubel Shelly & John O. York

Then Paul stood in front of the Areopagus and said, "Athenians, I see how extremely religious you are in every way. For as I went through the city and looked carefully at the objects of your worship, I found among them an altar with the inscription, 'To an unknown god.' What therefore you worship as unknown, this I proclaim to you. The God who made the world and everything in it, he who is Lord of heaven and earth, does not live in shrines made by human hands, nor is he served by human hands, as though he needed anything, since he himself gives to all mortals life and breath and all things. From one ancestor he made all nations to inhabit the whole earth, and he allotted the times of their existence and the boundaries of the places where they would live, so that they would search for God and perhaps grope for him and find him—though indeed he is not far from each one of us" (Acts 17:22-27, NRSV).

Between Athens and Jerusalem

We both live in Nashville, Tennessee—a city sometimes called the "buckle of the Bible Belt." Closer to our own backgrounds and religious tradition, Nashville is sometimes referred to jokingly as the "Jerusalem for Churches of Christ." But our city is better known outside of church settings as the "Athens of the South." We have our own Parthenon downtown, a replica of the Athenian original. The city hosts several universities and prides itself in Athens-like opportunities for education available to its citizens. We are also "Music City," of course, home to the Grand Ole Opry, birthplace of country music, and the heartland of contemporary Christian music.

One who visits Nashville for the first time, however, will also be impressed by the number of churches, many across the street from one another or immediately beside one another. At our location, the property adjoins Glen Leven United Presbyterian Church and faces Cofers Chapel Freewill Baptist Church. From any high vantage point in our county, what one immediately sees are church steeples dotting the landscape. There are over 100 Churches of Christ in Nashville, and hundreds upon thousands of other churches of myriad denominational or community church connections. We have a number of synagogues located throughout the city, and the Catholic Church is well represented. In recent years, we have become a city with international flavor as temples from the various world religions have been built in Nashville.

There are, of course, other sides to life in Nashville. An enormous socio-economic gulf exists between the rich and the poor, and an undercurrent of racial tension simmers barely beneath the surface. A prominent billboard advertises "The World's Largest Adult Bookstore" in our beloved city.

Curiously, for all of the high visibility of churches and religious talk and music in our city, recent surveys suggest that church attendance in Nashville is about the same as other cities our size across the nation. Those who do attend have become accustomed to driving past a dozen or more other churches to attend the church of their choice.

The words of Paul to the Athenians don't sound too distant from our own Athens of the South: "I see how extremely religious you are." That is the bad news and the good news of the circumstances in which we find ourselves—not just in Nashville but throughout the larger Christian community in America. The bad news is that there are too many buildings with too many people who can't talk to one another in the name of Jesus while seeking to wear the name *Christian* in some form or fashion.

> *Division has done more to hide Christ from the view of men than all the infidelity that has ever been spoken.*
>
> —George MacDonald

Like the Athenians of Paul's day, we are a very religious people; aside from our own religious practices, however, we have lived too long as though God was unknown and no longer active in our world or in our lives. For many the Christian faith and traditional-institutional structures no longer hold much more than cultural or social significance. Even in our churches, we are hungering for the God who is largely unknown to us—but who is near us nonetheless.

Yet, right in the midst of this malaise, we sense that God is breaking in on our Athens/Jerusalem just as he did in the first century. At the beginning of the twenty-first century, there is a longing for spirituality and community that wasn't present just a few years ago. There is a hunger for God and the experience of relationship with God and God's people that is breaking through the cultural, social, and denominational barriers that created the divided church world of our prior experience. People want to believe in *the God who is not far from each one of us.*

We Have Been Here Before

When Jesus was born at what proved to be a "hinge point" to history, the *Pax Romana* held sway, widespread travel was possible because Roman roads and seas had been reclaimed from brigands and pirates, and universal communication was feasible since Greek was the common tongue of the civilized (i.e., Mediterranean) world. The main threat to Rome was not from any single geopolitical entity but from occasional uprisings of a guerilla or terrorist sort.

Similarly, our world is not embroiled in a major hot or cold war—although, as in the first Christian century, tensions exist on a smaller-but-still-very-frightening scale among ethnic, religious, and geographical groups. Travel is relatively easy and common—although encumbered by heavier security and a new degree of apprehension in the post-9/11 world—throughout the developed countries of the world. And the Internet has tied the global community together for instantaneous communication of data.

The most intriguing similarities between Jesus' time and our own run still deeper. They have to do not so much with political, social, and economic conditions as with the spiritual state of the world. Philosophy and religion have largely failed people, and they are casting about for something substantive that can give meaning to fragmented lives. Like the religious life Paul witnessed in Athens, there is much that is religious in our time; but "doing church" is not satisfying the hunger welling up from within. We do have a time in which the city of Nashville is unified on occasional Sundays in autumn, but the event that brings people together is Tennessee Titans football at the coliseum.

A yellowed piece of newspaper stuck in a file folder over twenty-five years ago now raises the fascinating possibility that the time of Jesus' birth parallels our own point in history. It was an interview with the late Will Durant, the Pulitzer Prize-winning author whose *The Story of Philosophy* and ten-volume *The Story of Civilization* are still widely circulated. In light of the cultural and intellectual shifts about to be made in the world when the comments were made, it almost seems prophetic.

> We are in the stage in which Greece was [sic] when the gods ceased to be gods and became mere poetry, and therefore exercised no element of order or command upon human behavior. There was the development of city life, of science and philosophy and the result was a period of pagan license—say around 200 B.C. to 100 A.D.—in which morals floundered in an ocean of competing religions, just as you have a flotsam and jetsam of religions today.
>
> By the time of Caesar you had a permissive society and a pagan society in the sense of sexual enjoyment with a minimal moral restraint. Now whether we shall have to wait for a new religion, the way the Greeks and Romans did, because... because what

happened was the old civilization decayed to the point where it cried out for a new religion, for something to worship and obey.[1]

Durant, though a Roman Catholic seminarian early in his life, died an agnostic. He nevertheless admitted that the advent of Christianity became "the supernatural basis for a new civilization which has lasted to the present." He wondered aloud in the interview if Christianity had "lost its hold" or whether it might yet "recover and there'll be a religious revival" in the world.

> *God offers to every mind its choice between truth and repose. Take which you please; you can never have both.*
>
> –Ralph Waldo Emerson

Interesting questions, are they not? And we are now at the point where it may be possible at least to speculate about an answer to them.

As a worldview, Modernity led western civilization down a dead-end street. Its doubt and cynicism threw out moral restraints. Its deification of science led to the jettisoning of biblical faith. There was little need for God, since science and human reason could discover all the useful knowledge available to our world. Paul's language of "shrines made with human hands" took on new meaning in our age of technology. At the close of the twentieth century, however, naïve arrogance about the world we were creating for ourselves gave way to fear and confusion. Young people dropped out and turned on to drugs. The exaltation of individual rights challenged all forms of social cohesion. Marriage came under attack as an institution, and out-of-wedlock births skyrocketed, creating massive social problems. With the failure of the Christian religion to address these situations successfully with a clear and certain word, Eastern religions became all the rage. Academic philosophy lamented its inability to contribute anything but analysis to what was going on. These same phenomena were playing themselves out in the world into which Christianity was born originally.

Postmodernity

Now a Postmodern worldview has emerged that practically cries out for a bold articulation of the same essential features of faith that turned the world upside down in the generation after Jesus' death. Turns in both science and philosophy have people speaking freely of the possibility—even probability—of divine presence in the universe. To say the least, an arrogant and contemptuous wave of the hand against the Christian faith is no longer necessary or even fashionable. Even government-sponsored social programs aimed at crime, poverty, AIDS, and teen pregnancy now partner with churches to fund "faith-based initiatives."

Postmodernism is quick to deny the Enlightenment assumption that only data that can be known through the five senses can be counted as relevant to the human condition. Human rational capacities are no longer deemed ultimate. Thus a Postmodern world is more open to the Christian claim that there are metaphysical truths that reach beyond what can be discerned by reason. These truths are neither irrational nor anti-rational. They are supra-rational.

Postmodernity also challenges the notion of "objective, dispassionate knowledge" from which the knower disengages himself. It affirms instead that observers never stand outside the historical process. We participate in history, culture, and language. Thus we are more than cognitive animals. We function holistically as body, mind, emotions, and spirit. Hardly any word gets more play in a Postmodern world, in fact, than the term "spiritual."

Is everything lovely and inviting about Postmodernism from a Christian standpoint? *By no means!* It is highly relativistic and tends to rank all human interpretations of history's narrative as both equally correct and equally flawed. Historic Christianity makes exclusivistic claims about the role of Jesus of Nazareth and would never permit the gospel to be offered on the smorgasbord of world religions. No more than Paul could be satisfied for Jesus to be absorbed into the Roman pantheon of gods can modern apologists accept so little for him. "For even if there are so-called gods, whether in heaven or on earth (as indeed there are many 'gods' and many 'lords'), yet for us there is but one God, the Father, from whom all things came and for whom we live; and there is but one Lord, Jesus Christ, through whom all things came and through whom we live" (1 Cor. 8:5-6; cf. John 14:6; Acts 4:12; 1 John 2:23).

At the same time, Paul's words to the Athenians provide an interesting model for reflecting on our own circumstances. Rather than telling these pagan Athenians how far removed they are from God, he explains how near God is. Rather than denouncing all of their behaviors, he reflects on the activity of God in making himself known through Christ. Rather than attempting to get them to "think" right, he seeks to include them in the great story of Creator God who has now acted in Jesus to draw all humanity to himself.

A Starting Point

So how do we make the case for the Christian story in our new world? It can no longer be an intellectual exercise of establishing merely the data and the logic of a "system." Instead, we believe that the good news must be enfleshed again. At the hinge-point of history some 2,000 years ago, the Word became flesh in the person and life of Jesus. In our own time, the Word must become flesh in the members of Christ's spiritual body, the church. The gospel must be seen and experienced relationally in authentic living.

Rather than attempting to out-argue other philosophical and religious points of view, the truth claims of our faith must be experienced in the flesh-and-blood daily lives of people who exist in the spiritual power and presence of the Lord. Perhaps it is time to hear afresh the invitation of Jesus to "come and see" where he is abiding (John 1:38-39). The Psalmist put it this way: "Taste and see that the LORD is good" (Psalm 34:8). The appeal we are making in this volume is summarized well by Paul: "Therefore, I urge you, brothers, in view of God's mercy, to offer your bodies as living sacrifices, holy and pleasing to God–this is your spiritual act of worship.... For the kingdom of God is not a matter of eating and drinking, but of righteousness, peace and joy in the Holy Spirit" (Rom.12:1; 14:17a).

> *How very good and pleasant it is when kindred live together in unity!*
>
> – Psalm 133:1

The Unity of the Body of Christ

The goal of this book is to address only one of the many issues raised by this Modern-to-Postmodern paradigm shift—the possibility for meaningful unity among those who make an orthodox confession of Jesus Christ as the Son of God. We believe that this worldview shift is another of those "hinge points" in history, and that God is calling his church to be the living body of Christ today in refreshing, energizing ways. We believe the divisive attitude of Christians toward one another that dominated the past couple of centuries has been more a cultural phenomenon demanded by the worldview of Modernity than a righteous phenomenon demanded by Scripture. Specifically, we believe it was the inevitable result of an institutional view of Christianity and a distinctly American way of reading the Bible. We want to propose instead a more relational model for how those who profess love for Jesus Christ should relate to him and to one another.

We do not speak of "creating" or "achieving" the unity of Christ's spiritual body. To the contrary, we use New Testament language of "making every effort to *maintain* the unity of the Spirit in the bond of peace" (Eph.4:3). The oneness of Christ's church is—like forgiveness, eternal life, and every other spiritual gift—a divine creation deposited among us by grace. We have simply not respected, honored, and maintained it. We have chosen to elevate persons, interpretations, and denominations above Jesus. We have been guilty of a none-too-subtle idolatry of exalting our "issues" to a greater significance than our Savior. The proof of this claim lies in the religious partisanship and sectarianism witnessed throughout Christendom.

Our goal is to explore, experience, and offer a proposal for Christian unity that is so thoroughly Jesus-centered that it will commend itself to thoughtful believers from many quarters. We are not so arrogant as to think anything here is definitive. Others can refine and clarify the concept. Others will experience what we dream about more fully than we shall ever understand. If we can contribute only a small part to the quest, we will have realized our goal completely. If we can help our readers grasp the precious truth that God is not far from us, perhaps we can discover together the reality of his presence in holy, loving, and healing community. Perhaps we can cut through the prison bars of religious institutionalism and begin living the liberated, joyous life of Christ.

Note: Because the chapters in this book are adaptations of material originally presented by the two of us in a series of sermons preached for the Family of God at Woodmont Hills in Nashville, we were presented with the challenge of trying to use "we" language throughout versus occasional first-person narrative. Because of the practical difficulties involved, we have chosen to indicate the primary author for each chapter. The overall thesis has been developed in concert. The individual chapters have been written by the author indicated, then reviewed and occasionally expanded by the other.

Note

1. James M. Doyle, "Writing Couple Believes World in Decline Peril," (Memphis) *Commercial Appeal* (Dec. 4, 1977), Sec. C, p. 6.

For one sect then to say,
Ours is the true Church, and
another say, Nay, but ours
is the true Church, is as
mad as to dispute whether
your hall or kitchen, or
parlor, or coal-house is
your house, and for one
to say, This is the house,
and another, Nay, but it
is that; when a child can
tell them, that the best
is but a part, and the house
containeth them all.

–Richard Baxter

2. Why Satan Loves Churches

John O. York

Conversation. It's what we humans have with each other to communicate. We talk to one another. We also have an amazing capacity to forget almost everything we say and hear. Some of it, in my case at least, is a matter of bad listening skills. We human beings don't always pay attention to what people are saying. Sometimes the most important people in our lives say things we just don't "hear." There are other conversations that we really wish we could remember, but they are soon lost in the sounds and busyness of life.

We do, of course, remember some conversations. The words may have been spoken years ago, but they had such impact on our lives that we still remember them almost word for word. For some reason, many of mine have occurred on airline travels. Conversations with strangers, some of them people whose names I never learned. One in particular that I can remember very distinctly occurred in 1988.

Our Familiar Divisions

I was flying from Atlanta to Detroit. The plane was not crowded; I had a window seat and there was a man sitting in the aisle seat reading a magazine when I sat down. The plane had barely cleared the runway when he handed his magazine to me and asked me if I'd ever seen "that" as he pointed to the picture. It was an old car, the make and model of which I had no idea. He told me it was a Tucker. I later learned that the magazine article he was reading coincided with a movie released in 1988 called *Tucker: The Man and His Dream.* This stranger was more than willing to tell me about the car and the movie as our flight continued.

The conversation changed, however, when he began to inquire about my destination for the day and my background. No, I wasn't flying to Detroit; that was an intermediate stop.

"What do you do?" I explained that I was a teacher at a small private college.

"What field?"

"Religion," I responded.

"Oh," he said, "what church?"

"Churches of Christ."

"Ah, the people who think they're the only ones going to heaven! My father and my uncle haven't spoken to each other for thirty years because of the Church of Christ. My father's family was raised Baptist. And when my uncle married a woman from the Church of Christ, he had to convert. They haven't spoken to each other since."

Perhaps you've had those conversations as well. Or perhaps the bruises and beatings—spiritual, emotional, and even physical—have come through other sorts of experiences with church and supposedly churched people. Too many of us know first-hand the problems with Christ's fragmented church.

So why is it that our attempts to be the body of Christ in our time so often fail? Why is it that when confronted with the temptations of power and control over people, and sometimes even service to others, we humans don't manage the circumstances nearly as well as Jesus did? Think for a moment about the temptations of Jesus when he was first driven by the Spirit into the wilderness.

Jesus, full of the Holy Spirit, returned from the Jordan and was led by the Spirit in the wilderness, where for forty days he was tempted by the devil. He ate nothing at all during those days, and when they were over, he was famished. The devil said to him, "If you are the Son of God, command this stone to become a loaf of bread." Jesus answered him, "It is written, 'One does not live by bread alone.'" Then the devil led him up and showed him in an instant all the kingdoms of the world. And the devil said to him, "To you I will give their glory and all this authority; for it has been given over to me, and I give it to anyone I please. If you, then, will worship me, it will all be yours." Jesus answered him, "It is written, 'Worship the Lord your God, and serve only him.'"

Then the devil took him to Jerusalem, and placed him on the pinnacle of the temple, saying to him, "If you are the Son of God, throw yourself down from here, for it is written, 'He will command his angels concerning you, to protect you,' and 'On their hands they will bear you up, so that you will not dash your foot against a stone.'" Jesus answered him, "It is said, 'Do not put the Lord your God to the test.'" When the devil had finished every test, he departed from him until an opportune time (Luke 4:1-12).

Jesus immediately understood that solving his own hunger, even demonstrating his capacity to solve world hunger, was not his prerogative; it is God's. He immediately recognized the devil's efforts to entice him to choose power and authority (the kingdoms of the world) or to demonstrate his divine superiority (jumping from the pinnacle of the temple) as denials of God the Father's sovereign rule in his life. With his death and resurrection and the promised pouring out of the Spirit (Acts 2; cf. John 14-16, 20), disciples of Jesus were given that same presence which drove Jesus into the wilderness.

> *[I pray] that they may all be one. As you, Father, are in me and I am in you, may they also be in us, so that the world may believe that you have sent me.*
>
> –John 17:21

One cannot read very long in Acts or work through Paul's letters without discovering that Satan wasted little time in trying to recover from his defeat at the cross. The first "scandal" in the church was a direct result of Satan's efforts. When Ananias and Sapphira sold property and gave only part of the proceeds to the apostles (while claiming to give it all), Peter confronted them with these words: "Ananias, why has Satan filled your heart to lie to the Holy Spirit and keep back part of the proceeds of the land?" (Acts 5:3). From that time to the present, Satan has been working hard to strip the promise of life from those already called by God.

A Satanic Strategy: Division

In 1941, from May 2 to November 28, the late C. S. Lewis wrote a series of imaginary letters for a weekly religious newspaper in England called *The Guardian*. The letters were later collected in a book entitled *The Screwtape Letters*. Screwtape was the name Lewis gave to a high-level agent of Satan. He was writing to his apprentice demon Wormwood, giving advice on Wormwood's efforts to keep the human assigned to him from going over to the enemy—God. Here's how the second chapter begins:

> My dear Wormwood—I note with grave displeasure that your patient has become a Christian. Do not indulge the hope that you will escape the usual penalties; indeed, in your better moments, I trust you would hardly even wish to do so. In the meantime we must make the best of the situation. There is no need to despair; hundreds of these adult converts have been reclaimed after a brief sojourn in the Enemy's camp and are now with us. All the habits of the patient, both mental and bodily, are still in our favor. One of our great allies at present is the Church itself.[1]

Screwtape then goes on to give a series of suggestions for using the new Christian's experience of church and churched people to nullify all of his newfound faith convictions. You can guess the issues to be highlighted: the meaningless, dull worship; the hypocrites sitting down the row.

At one point Screwtape encourages Wormwood to get his patient to focus on a particular theological conviction. Since these letters were written in the midst of World War II, Screwtape suggests that the patient become consumed with either *pacifism* or fighting a *just war*. He doesn't care which side the patient takes so long as he becomes consumed with his conviction to the point that he believes his position is the only faithful response. At that point, Screwtape argues, the conviction will become the faith—thus supplanting the Enemy as the true object of his trust and devotion.

Isn't it true that almost any good can be twisted into something evil? In the history of Christian thought, the idea of *Sola Scriptura*—Scripture alone as the basis for faith and understanding—seemed like a necessary corrective to a historic belief that church tradition and church authorities had either equal or superior authority. The development of the printing press and the ability of everyone to have his own copy of Scripture certainly was better than having Scripture only in the hands of a few official church interpreters.

The modern era—the Age of Reason we have called it, the rise of scientific method, and the belief that every individual human is capable of thinking and deciding for him- or herself—surely that was an improvement over earlier times of illiteracy and ignorance among the masses of humanity on our planet. Life after Copernicus and Galileo and Sir Isaac Newton surely is an improvement—knowing that the universe is ordered and can be studied and that we humans have the capacity for collecting the data, the facts, thereby coming to understand truth in our world. We can't turn back the clock to days before modern medicine and vaccines that can virtually wipe out diseases like polio, or to a time before our access to all the ancient manuscripts and the ability to produce modern translations of Scripture

You may already sense where we're going with these examples. "Scripture Only" can easily be turned into bibliolatry—worship of the book itself or a particular translation. Having multiple copies of Scripture in every home in America is not a sign of biblical literacy but of biblical apathy in many cases. The Age of Reason—with its emphasis on individualism—means that each of us is responsible for coming to his or her own version of the truth. And time has now demonstrated that practically everyone, indeed, has his or her own version. Thus the forces that created the Protestant Reformation and the nineteenth-century American Restoration Movement simply multiplied division—though both affirmed the unity of true believers in Christ as a primary goal and driving force!

The more individualized we have become and the more certainty with which we believed we could objectively know truth, the more divided the church that Christ died for has become. The denominational world of our experience in America is directly tied to the belief that each of us can read and study the Bible for himself and arrive at the same truths of Scripture. "Do away with human creeds," we said. "Speak where the Bible speaks, and be silent where the Bible is silent." But the slogan was as human centered and as individualistically interpreted as those creeds we denounced.

> *Church unity is like peace, we are all for it, but we are not willing to pay the price.*
>
> –Willem A. Visser't Hooft

Just get us humans more interested in our differences and distinctions than in our common ground and similarities in Christ, and the church remains the devil's playground.

Living With a New Paradigm

Meanwhile, at the dawn of the twenty-first century, the world has shifted. The certainty with which we understood the laws of nature and the science of objective truth have been undermined by new discoveries. The age of technology, with its notion of our universe as one giant well-oiled machine, has been confronted with some new realities. One writer puts it this way:

> With the development of quantum physics, we discovered a world that did not behave the way Newton said it should. It was impossible to pin down, with waves turning into particles and particles into waves. What had mass one moment was pure energy the next, and none of it was predictable. The very act of observing a particle changed its behavior, which destroyed the whole notion of scientific objectivity. A scientist could not stand outside the world to watch it. The same particles that were busy responding to each other responded to the watcher as well, revealing a world that was not made up of manageable things but of constantly changing relationships. It is no longer possible to think of the world as a machine.[2]

What does any of that say about the future of denominations and hair-splitting divisions in the church? In the world of institutional church—where the church was viewed as a giant machine—the pursuit of a "better church machine" seemed to make sense. The selling of the church with slogans and slick advertising was a logical extension of evangelism. As long as we thought about being Christian in individualistic terms, as long as the focus was on ourselves and *my* worship preferences and *my* church group and *my* view of baptism and *my* rules for making melody with the heart—as long as we continued to choose the church of our own making and preference, such divisions were inevitable. And the church continued to be a great ally of Satan.

But what if the church is not a machine? What if objective truth isn't so scientifically objective at all? What if the goal is not to have all of the right answers to Bible trivia questions? What if the goal is not to be doctrinally sound? What if, in a relational model, people once again focus on the Christ instead of each group's particular set of proof texts and practices? What if all that looks so random actually is relational?

What happens if we stop viewing the church as an institution or thinking of the church mechanistically? For example, people sometimes describe our worship services as "well-oiled machines." Perhaps what they mean by that is an endorsement of the comfort and security that comes from knowing exactly what's going to happen next. Fit it all into a neat and clean one-hour package; take precisely eight minutes for the Lord's Supper, etc. You see, in a machine you know (or at least rely on the assumption) that every part works the same way every time. Thus the comfort of a worship assembly that feels and looks the same every time. The comfort and security of having the rules for church. The comfort and security of a diagram with neat circles. Everyone is in a closed system with circles to define who belongs and who doesn't. One may not always know who is in or out, but we can all assure ourselves that *we are in*, right?

In the earliest days of the church, heresy was defined by Paul and John, at least, as a decision to believe in something other than the all-sufficiency of Christ. Anyone who claimed special knowledge accessible only to the spiritual elite was a heretic (Col. 2-3). Anyone who denied Jesus as God having come in the flesh was a heretic (1 John 2). Anyone demanding that particular human performances were prerequisites for faith was heretical (Gal. 1-3). Anyone who became more enamored with the material world and the security of possessions over faith in the invisible God was heretical (Acts 5; apparently Demas in 2 Tim. 4:10). They all shared in common the decision that Christ alone was not enough. To be in the group one also had to know this or that, do this or that.

Conclusion

Satan's games haven't changed since then. But here is the enormously good news in our time. We're convinced that the days of sectarianism are gone or at least numbered. Most people have no loyalties or allegiances to such labels. They are sick of hairsplitting, doctrinaire conversations, tired of the arrogance of our modern world that believed only the material world was real. We long to believe in the spiritual, in truth that is above reason, in the mystery of a universe that cannot be contained by our finite understandings. We long to encounter the mystery of God in our world, in our lives.

Yes, Satan already is at work twisting that human longing for spirituality into all kinds of faddish, superficial pursuits. Yes, you will hear many church leaders rail against the heresy of Postmodernism and others bitterly complaining that truth is no longer objective. Some of their fears will be founded, precisely because good can always be twisted into evil. Let us not be caught once more in the human name-and-blame game so that once again Satan takes our eyes off of Jesus. The time has come for Jesus to be glorified through us as we live in new and renewed relationship with him and his kingdom people.

No, this is not an appeal to slight Acts and the Epistles in our scripture loyalties in the name of giving emphasis to the four Gospel accounts. I do have a sneaking suspicion, however, that something of a reverse mistake was part of our modern efforts to get our church life correct. The decision to focus on Jesus will necessitate reading *all* of Scripture again[3] to see how God is at work in our world and our lives. We will read the New Testament letters and Acts in an effort to discover how first-century Christians sought to be Jesus in their time. Our focus of interpretation will thus shift from a judicial search for the rules of human behavior lifted out of "God's rule book" to a relational pursuit of being the living body of Christ in our own time. This will call for fresh eyes and strong hearts of faith as we rethink what it means to be Jesus (rather than just talk about Jesus) in our time.

Notes

1. C.S. Lewis, *The Screwtape Letters* (New York: Macmillan & Co., 1961), p. 15.

2. Barbara Brown Taylor, "Preaching into the Next Millennium," *Exilic Preaching*, ed. by Erskine Clark (Harrisburg, PA: Trinity International, 1998), p. 92. For a more detailed account of the changes in worldview now upon us, see Robert Webber, *Ancient-Future Faith: Rethinking Evangelicalism for*

a Postmodern World (Grand Rapids: Baker Books, 1999), pp. 13-38; Brian McLaren, *A New Kind of Christian* (San Francisco: Jossey-Bass, 2001), pp. 14-19; Tony Jones, *Postmodern Youth Ministry* (Grand Rapids: Zondervan/ Youth Specialties, 2001), pp. 9-43.

3. This means taking seriously Paul's words to Timothy that the "sacred writings" (clearly the Hebrew Scriptures in that context) instructed him in the way of salvation (2 Tim. 3:14ff.). It also means reading Scripture as a living Word from God, not merely an ancient historical artifact, that is the revelation of God himself and authoritative vision for life lived in fellowship with him. With the author of Hebrews, we will read all of Scripture through the lens of God's revelation of himself in Jesus Christ.

Christianity is not,
and never has been,
about finding the right
combination of words!
It is about
encountering the living
and loving God.

–Alister E. McGrath

If we would but observe
unity in essentials,
liberty in non-essentials,
charity in all things,
our affairs would
certainly be in the best
possible situation.

–Robert Maldenius

3. THERE IS AN ALTERNATIVE

John O. York

Paul's exhortation to the Philippian church seems so simple and straightforward:

> If then there is any encouragement in Christ, any consolation from love, any sharing in the Spirit, any compassion and sympathy, make my joy complete: be of the same mind, having the same love, being in full accord and of one mind. Do nothing from selfish ambition or conceit, but in humility regard others as better than yourselves. Let each of you look not to your own interests, but to the interests of others. Let the same mind be in you that was in Christ Jesus. (Phil. 2:1-5)

Likewise, his words of instruction to the Ephesians calling them to maintain the unity of the Spirit in the bond of peace are not difficult to comprehend. Equipping the saints for ministry, "building up the body of Christ, until all of us come to the unity of the faith and of the knowledge of the Son of God, to maturity, to the measure of the full stature of Christ" (Eph. 4:12-13). There are no textual or translation issues clouding the meaning of the text. There is some comfort, I suppose, in realizing that these words were written in the first place precisely because unity among believers was not a given. "Having the same mind" was not easy nor was it the common outcome among believers even in the earliest days of belief in Jesus Messiah.

> *We are not to make men converts of our opinions. But we are to make them disciples of Jesus.*
>
> –Oswald Chambers

In our own time, we are painfully aware of Christianity in America. It is filled not only with stories of religious freedom and toleration but also stories of religious intolerance, stories of prejudice and abuse, stories of division and isolation. It infects all of the denominations. A sectarian spirit disrupts the body of Christ. The same spirit marks my own heritage within the American Restoration Movement of the nineteenth century, with its early focus on unity that eventually dissolved into a wide spectrum of divided churches and divisive practices.

The Unity Challenge

So what makes this unity business so difficult? Why didn't that lofty goal of speaking where the Bible speaks and being silent where the Bible is silent produce something other than more division? Why did Paul's exhortation to unity become a demand for doctrinal uniformity, where "my way" is the right way and where unity will come just as soon as you see Scripture and church and worship—especially worship—my way?

Recently I received a shipment of books that had belonged to my grandfather. At the time the books arrived, he was almost ninety-five years old and his mental and physical health were both in rapid decline. He was under full-time care in a nursing home, and since has died. So the family had begun the process of sorting through his belongings. All of the religious books came to my family, for the use of his grandson and his great-grandsons.

Most of them were old commentary sets whose value is now greatly limited because the scholarship is outdated. There was an early copy of the Phillips translation of the New Testament; a copy of *Haley's Bible Handbook*; a book called *Preachers of Today*, which contains pictures and short biographical notes on preachers from the 1950s and early '60s. Then I came across *The Wallace-Vaughn Debate.*[1]

My grandfather wrote the date in this book when he purchased it—1960. The debate itself actually took place in 1951, and there is a preface that explains the circumstances. It's not difficult to discover who published the book. On one side of the debate was "Mr." Vaughn; on the other side of the debate was "Brother" Wallace. The debate itself was held over three successive evenings, September 5-7, 1951. The local high school auditorium in Arvada, Colorado, was rented for the occasion. Radio and newspaper advertising, as well as handbills carried door to door, informed the townspeople of the event.

At the time, Arvada was a town of about 2,350 people (today it is a suburb of Denver, with a population of over

104,000). It is worth noting that one's chances of getting a crowd for such an occasion were better in those days. The entertainment competition on Wednesday through Friday nights in a small town certainly was nothing like today.

Would you like to guess what these two men debated for three nights? Or why my grandfather not only bought the book ten years later but marked it and wrote notes in the margins? "Proposition: Resolved: 'That there is only one person in the Godhead and that Baptism is only in the name of the Lord Jesus.'" There were three nights of disputing, with Ray Vaughn affirming the proposition and G. K. Wallace denying it.

Actually, the first issue, if I understand it correctly, has some significance. Ultimately, the debate was over the nature of the relationship between God the Father, God the Son, and God the Holy Spirit. I had to read several pages before I realized what the second part of the debate was about. As in the Godhead discussion, each man's argument came down to proof-texts. One side argued on the basis of Matthew 28:19 ("baptizing in the name of the Father, the Son, and the Holy Spirit") and the other argued on the basis of Acts 2:38 ("be baptized...in the name of Jesus Christ"). This was not a debate between a believer and an atheist. This was a debate between believers, a Pentecostal preacher and a Church of Christ preacher.

Nothing is said in the preface about local outcomes. Did people come to know Christ from the experience? Were those outside the Christian faith positively inclined to Christ by the discussion? I wonder: Would anyone come out on a Wednesday, Thursday, or Friday evening in any month of this year for such a debate?

The Great Myth: *Our* Objectivity

My guess is that not everyone in Arvada, Colorado, was interested in the debate back in 1951. Even though I had not even been born that year, I can remember the urgent need to be right, the need to have an answer to every Bible trivia question, the need to know that we were members of the group that had the right answers. Rubel and I can both remember when evangelism was a matter of convincing other church-going people that they were wrong and we were right. We both remember when there was great comfort and no small amount of identity invested in knowing that our reading of Scripture and our patterns for the worship assembly and our understanding of the human activities required for salvation were obvious to anyone who could see beyond his or her prejudices.

It never really crossed our minds that we might also have prejudices and subjectivity! Why, we can even remember the days of our youth when people said that our churches were the fastest-growing in America. Three decades later, it would be discovered that the numbers generated in the 1960s suffered from the same accounting problems as several now-infamous corporations in the past few years.

So what became of the plea for unity? For that matter, what happened to evangelism? Is it that we all just became lazy? Did we all become intimidated by our culture or stop caring that other people were lost eternally? Did some of us become embarrassed by our own church experiences to the point that we didn't want to ask anyone to come to church with us? Did the world around us become so hard of hearing that it was pointless to talk to them? Did we decide with the pop psychologists of the '70s that "I'm okay, you're okay"—so it really doesn't matter what one believes about God or his son Jesus? Did we opt for social concerns and financial security to the point of neglecting spirituality? Did we choose feeling good about ourselves over keeping the commands of God?

At the beginning of the twenty-first century, we seem to be faced with a difficult dichotomy. If we choose unity, we must sacrifice the need to be right—which in the end is experienced as a violation of conscience. If we choose unity, we must sacrifice our commitments to the Lord's Supper or to *a cappella* music or to baptism. On the other hand, if we choose our need to be right on every point of doctrine, we sacrifice unity and are accused of being sectarian.

Meanwhile we live in a world in which the questions seldom seem to fit our answers. It is that second path—the pursuit of the right answer to every point of doctrine—that seems so out of step. In this new perspective that we have been calling Postmodernity, the collection of facts and data and intellectual right answers has grown cold and sterile. Those debate questions with their syllogisms and mental gymnastics have been replaced by a desire to experience reality with our whole person.[2] We finally realized that we could not know God with our brains alone. All of the right answers in the world didn't necessarily make us better people. That was the problem in our twentieth-century world. We had more knowledge than ever before, but that did not make us better people.

Likewise in our churches, having all right answers on Sunday in church did not erase the contradictions of our lives. It didn't seem to make us more loving. We did not become less egocentric. Bigotry and racism did not disappear. Plus, we became increasingly uneasy with those tight definitions that separated our church life from the rest of life. Worship, by definition, had to be confined to our large corporate assemblies because that was the only way to make sense of our right answers about *a cappella* music. People had to understand our precise language about "baptism for the remission of sins" because we kept bumping into people whose lives exemplified the fruit of the Spirit but whose answers about baptism did not match our own.

Still, there was the matter of our right reading of Scripture that none of us wished to sacrifice. Deep down in our own hearts, we realized that knowing the right answers did not make one a Christian. We thought our interpretation of Scripture was just simple, open-minded reading of the facts. But when one collects data in search of patterns for human behavior, Scripture is reduced to a series of propositions and the larger story is lost. Thus, when the reading of Scripture was narrowed to the pattern for the church and for the patterns of worship—even patterns of ethical behavior—we performed the same short-cut on Scripture that we use all of the time now in computer databases. We understand that what we put into our computer search automatically determines what can come out. The same is true when we use that methodology on the text.

> *Accept one another, then, just as Christ accepted you, in order to bring praise to God.*
>
> –Romans 15:7

In the mental processing of proof-texts for our particular search questions, we sometimes lost sight of Jesus. We replaced relationship with God and with one another with the human confidence that we had the right answers. We then built church relationships around our right answers. We chose the church whose answers best conformed to our own. We converted outsiders to our right answers. We brought people into our right worship practices. We created social relationships that served as our cultural-religious network called church. We created faith in our own right answers and practices.

Thus, there is great fear in our time of those "change agents" who would alter our worship styles and make adjustments to our doctrines of the Lord's Supper or baptism or the role of women in our assemblies. When *faith* is in the right answers and *community* is formed around the right answers and *unity* must be maintained by keeping the right answers intact, then even the slightest change in style is a change of content. It is an attack on faith itself.

The Rediscovery of Grace

In our own fellowship, it was the rediscovery of grace that began to erode our must-have-the-right-answers mentality, our debate-the-other-believers mentality. Salvation was God's gift, not our performance and a correct set of right answers. Grace meant we were saved by God's activity, not our own. Grace was the means of overcoming the growing contradictions of our lives. Grace recognized that our sinful behavior wasn't being prevented or fixed by having the right answers and being able to win every argument. Grace was the gift of God, the activity of God in our lives. Grace opened the door of heaven to the rest of our human lives, allowing us to bring our emotions and our bodies back into the church building. As long as our intellectual understanding of right answers and right performances determined "sound faith and practice," there could be no variance in our experiences of worship.

Grace allowed us to stop demanding that unity be uniformity of thought. Grace meant that we no longer had to shoot our wounded. Church could become a confessional people again, where we told the truth about our messed up lives instead of gathering and acting as if we are all perfect with all of our right church answers and all of our right church practices.

Grace allowed us to hear the language of relationship afresh. Grace allowed us to experience spirituality as relationship with God. It allowed us to reconsider the possibility that we could have relationship with other people—even when they don't think exactly like we think. After all, it is by grace that we have been saved, not by our performance or our right answers. That surely must be true of others, not just our little minority in the world of Christ-followers.

But at times grace became a new right answer to fight about. It was even an escapist right answer for some, without the simultaneous recognition that we also are empowered by God's Holy Spirit to live transformed lives. It is that Holy Spirit presence that makes us God's sacred space on this planet. It is the empowering Spirit that leads us beyond the contradiction of continuing to sin that grace may abound. It is the empowering Spirit that demands our whole person be engaged relationally with God and with one another. Mind cannot be separated from body or soul. Worship cannot be segregated into an hour-long intellectual performance on Sunday morning when the Spirit of God is ever-present, when we are the living temple of God.

Yes, we are indeed blessed to live in a world that no longer thinks God can be apprehended by brain-power alone. Yes, we still confess the Bible as the Word of God, but a way has been opened to us to stop reading as the Pharisees read. Scripture is the story of God actively at work in his creation, at work in Christ to restore humanity to the relational living intended in the Garden of Eden. Spirituality is no longer the quest for religious facts collected and held as true by our brains and then practically acted upon in a series of performances. It's not what you go do on Sunday anymore. It is connected again to the whole person—intellect, emotions, body movements, lifestyle.

The Quest for Community in Christ

There is a longing for relationship and connection today that will not tolerate exclusivist claims. Ironically, any group claiming to be the only Christians in our time will become a self-fulfilling prophecy of sorts. Such intolerance will lead to an isolation that will become extinction.

> *Let us rejoice in the truth wherever we find its lamp burning.*
>
> –Albert Schweitzer

So how do we hear Paul's words about unity and sameness in our time? I'm not interested in creating a new "right answer," a better proof-text. Perhaps we begin by collectively reading the entire letter to the Philippians together rather than lifting out a few verses here and there. In order to understand the language of Paul's appeal to have "the same mind" in chapter two, we will have to hear his self-understanding of identity in chapter one. For

Paul, to live is Christ and thus to die is gain. It is his identity *in* Christ, his life consumed with imitating Christ, and his shared relationship with these people whom he loves *in* Christ, that empowers the calling to share the same mind, the same worldview that they have in common with Christ.

Paul's language of new creation is also used in other contexts. He no longer sees from a human point of view. Now, in Christ, everything is new creation. We live at a time in human history where people long for new creation. Those who believe in Jesus Messiah also long for new creation of this denominated, segregated, sectarian, compartmentalized church world. There is a great desire that the institutional structures we have labeled "church" heed the example of Jesus through death and resurrection.[3] We live in a world in which those words written almost 200 years ago in the "Last Will and Testament of the Springfield Presbytery" can be heard again:

> We will, that this body die, be dissolved, and sink
> into union with the Body of Christ at large; for there
> is but one Body, and one Spirit, even as we are called
> in one hope of our calling.[4]

Conclusion

The local church for which the two of us preach is consciously trying to continue to sink into union with the body of Christ at large. Yes, the body of Christ at large is always concretely expressed in local fellowships, in units of believers we call assemblies or local churches. But within particular communities of faith we can live again with a larger vision of ourselves beyond the boundaries that have dominated American Protestant Christianity. We can remember again that the real enemy is Satan, not everyone who has an opinion contrary to our own. We can find our identity *in Christ*, we can share relationship with God *in Christ*. By the power of the Holy Spirit within us, we can live *in Christ*. We can live out our calling in union with the Body of Christ at large.

What becomes of our "right answers" then? The activities themselves are freed to be whole-person experiences of God rather than merit badges of right thinking and right doing. Baptism is no longer a "command performance" that we have to think right about or it doesn't count. Baptism becomes a whole-person experience at the center of the process of our adoption as sons and daughters of God. We can move beyond the rules of observing the Lord's Supper to experiencing the body and blood of Christ as a shared communion.

We are freed to be God's sacred space on this planet, his holy temple, the living body of Christ empowered by his Holy Spirit—Jesus to our world. Rather than being bound to doctrinal answers that turn into exclusivist claims, we are opened again to relational living with the Godhead and with one another and we share the worldview (i.e., same mind) that we have in Christ Jesus. Instead of "going to church" on Sundays, we can share in communities of faith that empower us to be the church throughout the week.

The questions remain, however: Do we break through the boundaries of our current constituencies to fully participate in the larger whole? If we recognize the larger whole in God's kingdom, will our Church of Christ identity somehow be irreversibly lost? If the latter were to be true, are we willing to take that risk in the name of Jesus for the sake of his One Body? What might such an approach to Scripture and church life look like in our time?

Notes

1. *Wallace-Vaughn Debate* (Longview, WA: Telegram Sermons Book Company, 1952).

2. Tony Jones states the comparison this way: The modern value was "Rational: Descartes epitomizes the modern love of all things cognitive and intellectual. In the decades that followed the Enlightenment, the human brain was considered the apex of the evolutionary chain of God's creation. In either case, centuries of Christian mysticism were left behind in a quest to comprehend God." The corresponding postmodern value is "Experiential: Strong is our desire to experience, as opposed to simply reading or hearing about things. Obviously, interactive video games are big sellers with middle school and high school students, just as high adventure vacations are with the post-college crowd. A postmodern with an extra $50 is probably more likely to get a massage or go to a really nice restaurant than to spend it in a way her parents deem more practical." Jones lists a series of comparisons between modern and postmodern which are helpful: rational/experiential; scientific/spiritual; unanimity/ pluralistic; exclusive/relative; egocentric/altruistic; individualistic/communal; functional/creative; industrial/environmental; local/global; compartmentalized/holistic; relevant/ authentic. Especially important is the last comparison. "Relevant: The clarion call of growing churches over the last few decades has been to preach in ways that make the gospel relevant to people's day-to-day lives. For instance, a seeker-sensitive church decided not to put a cross in the worship center so not to offend newcomers. Authentic: Related to holism, authenticity is a valued commodity. Some have described this as a shift 'from being relevant to being real.' Today, the younger generations respond, 'Don't tell me how to apply this Bible passage to my life. Just tell me what it really means. I'll decide how to apply it.' That means preaching the whole Bible—contradictions, wars, infidelity, everything." *Postmodern Youth Ministry* (Grand Rapids: Zondervan, 2001), pp. 30-37.

3. See the provocative thesis of Michael Jinkins, *The Church Faces Death: Ecclesiology in a Post-Modern Context* (New York: Oxford University Press, 1999), pp. 28-32.

4. "Last Will and Testament of the Springfield Presbytery," in *Historical Documents Advocating Christian Union*, ed. Charles Alexander Young (Chicago: Christian Century, 1904), 20.

It is an inherent weakness of religion not to take offense at the segregation of God, to forget that the true sanctuary has no walls. Religion has often suffered from the tendency to become parochial, self-indulgent, self-seeking; as if the task were not to ennoble human nature but to enhance the power and beauty of its institutions or to enlarge the body of doctrines. It has often done more to canonize prejudices than to wrestle for truth; to petrify the sacred than to sanctify the secular.

–Abraham Heschel

4. THE JESUS PROPOSAL / PART 1

Rubel Shelly

I belong to a *family*—the Shelly family. My immediate family consists now of only Myra and me. Our three grown-and-married children and their mates, sons, and daughters are still family to us, even though we no longer live at the same address. Then there are our two families of origin. We see them less frequently than our children and grandchildren, but they still count as family to us. The notion of extended family widens still further to include aunts and uncles, nephews and nieces, cousins and other kin.

If you were to picture this concept of family I have been describing, you might draw a series of circles—each a bit larger than the one before. By the time you get from immediate through close to more distant, perhaps the edges of those circles would need to be increasingly fuzzy. There are certainly people no farther removed than the third or fourth ring that I have never met. I don't know their names. Why, I wouldn't recognize them as family when passing them in a shopping mall or greeting them in a church lobby. And they may be equally as unaware that I am, at least in some distant sense of biological connection, part of their larger family too.

Press the matter all the way back to Noah—even to Adam—and I suppose we derive the term we occasionally employ when referring to "the human family." But we certainly evidence very little of the true sense of a connected and loving family across human history. People who speak different languages, embrace different cultural heritages, and/or have skin of a different color seem more inclined to think "foreigner" rather than "family" of the other. Ethnocentrism has even tended to have these dissimilar groups looking upon one another with disdain.

> *He who begins by loving Christianity better than truth will proceed by loving his own sect of church better than Christianity and end in loving himself better than all.*
>
> –Coleridge

Does the Bible not affirm that humankind shares a common ancestry under God? (Acts 17:26). Was that fact not part of the earliest church's plea for seeing the gospel as a message to Jews and Gentiles alike? And wasn't that plea a fulfillment of our Lord's promise to create "one flock, one shepherd"? (John 10:16b). Do we not think in terms nowadays of a "shrinking planet" and "global village" in calling one another to such things as ecological responsibility and dismantling terrorist structures? So why don't we take the notion of church as *the family of God* seriously?

Family: **Alike** *and* **Different**

Go back to the opening comments of this chapter about my natural family—the people to whom I am related "by blood." Although we share genetic material, we are as notable for our differences as for our likenesses. Truth be told, we are likely more notable for the things that distinguish us than for the things that reveal us as family to outsiders. Now if I am standing with my two sons, nobody will question that we are family. People come up to one or another of us in public places and say things like this: "Pardon me for bothering you, but I'll bet I know your son (father/brother). You look so much alike!" People even make mistakes in identifying or addressing us, and we have to tell them, "I think you have me confused with my brother (dad/son)."

But it is very different with my two brothers. Stand the three of us in a line of ten males, and I seriously doubt you would think we were kin—much less brothers! Discounting for a moment the gray hair we all sport now, one of us has black hair, one red, and one brown. Our body builds are different. At a more personal level, our temperaments and tastes are not that much alike either. Perhaps the fact that we are not close in age to each other accounts for many of those differences. I sometimes tell people that our mom and dad had "three only children"—in view of the fact that there is such an age and personality gap among the three of us.

Suppose we represent distinct family groups by circles drawn on a piece of paper. How do you determine the circle to which each person belongs? Maybe some family members stand out as family members—like my sons and me. But others are as diverse as the three brothers I described. So what makes us brothers? Not your decision about circle-placement but relationship. We do share DNA. We did grow up in the same family. We are children of James and Lucille Shelly.

In Chapter 5, I will return to this illustration and will claim that we have relied on drawing neat "circles" within the body of Christ in order to define the church *institutionally*, when we should have been thinking and living *relationally*. I am far less concerned anymore to draw circles—or lines of any kind—that separate people who love, seek, and confess Jesus Christ. Does that person's relationship to Jesus imply anything for his relationship to me? For my attitude toward him? Even if we don't look alike? Or think alike? Or worship alike? Or articulate our views of the Holy Spirit, baptism, church organization, or the Lord's Supper alike?

Let me ask again: Why don't we take the notion of church as *the family of God* seriously? Must we affirm, maintain, and deepen the divisions within the church? Is there nothing embarrassing about religious tribalism—and the wars that have resulted from it? Is it necessary to water down the gospel message to regard men and women from other traditions within Christendom as brothers and sisters in Christ? Do we have to look alike to be family? Or might we not be as different as some of us are from other members of our natural families? Might we not be able to live in loving relationship with people who are bounded by different circles (i.e., denominations) we have drawn over time since the first Christian century?

My thesis is that certain types of division are wrong and offensive to Jesus Christ. His followers cannot have spiritual fellowship with those who do not confess him as their crucified and risen Lord, but those who make that common confession must begin to honor him by looking for ways to include rather than exclude one another. For the sake of a common witness against unbelief, we must learn to stand together in Christ.

In the experience of my youth in Churches of Christ, the appeal for people to "stand together in Christ" ultimately got around to an appeal for everyone else to leave their denominations, disavow understandings of biblical texts different from ours, and repudiate doctrines, worship elements, or polities different from ours. We were right, and unity would be achieved when everyone else recognized and admitted it. We would be united when they came where we were theologically, embracd the same worship forms we practiced, and gave up their false ways.

> *There is no more profound or more dangerous enemy to Christianity than anything which shrinks it and makes it narrow.*
>
> –Abbé Henri Huvelin

An Older Heritage

Yet within that historical heritage of less than a century ago, a common slogan was "Christians only, not the only Christians." The first part of the slogan was designed to call for unity within the core message of the gospel—what C. S. Lewis would later term "mere Christianity"; the second part was intended to repudiate the potential arrogance that could be heard as a claim to exclude believers within other Christian groups.

What is known to historians as the American Restoration Movement—with its three principal branches (i.e., divisions!)

of Disciples of Christ, Independent Christian Churches, and Churches of Christ—was launched as a unity movement within Protestantism. What irony there is to historians and what wry amusement there must be to God that this "unity movement" has become one of the most brittle and divisive elements of present-day Christianity.

One of the seminal documents of this movement was Thomas Campbell's *Declaration and Address* that was published in 1809. Bearing in mind that his use of the term "Church of Christ" in the document was not intended as a distinctive name for one group of believers over against others nor for a local congregation but as a descriptive term for all Christians (i.e., the spiritual body that belongs to Jesus Christ), here are a few of the basic propositions he advanced on behalf of a quest for unity:

> That the Church of Christ on earth is essentially, intentionally, and constitutionally one; consisting of all those in every place that profess their faith in Christ and obedience to him in all things according to the Scriptures, and that manifest the same by their tempers and conduct, and of none else; as none else can be truly and properly called Christians.
>
> That although the Church of Christ upon earth must necessarily exist in particular and distinct societies, locally separate from one another, yet there ought to be no schisms, no uncharitable divisions among them. They ought to receive each other as Christ Jesus hath received them, to the glory of God. And for this purpose they ought all to walk by the same rule, to mind and speak the same thing; and to

be perfectly joined together in the same mind, and in the same judgment.

That in order to do this, nothing ought to be inculcated upon Christians as articles of faith; nor required of them as terms of communion, but what is expressly taught and enjoined on them in the word of God....

That although inferences and deductions from Scripture premises, when fairly inferred, may be truly called the doctrine of God's holy word, yet are they not formally binding upon the consciences of Christians farther than they perceive the connection, and evidently see that they are so; for their faith must not stand in the wisdom of men, but in the power and veracity of God. Therefore no such deductions can be made terms of communion [i.e., fellowship, RS]....

That division among the Christians is a horrid evil, fraught with many evils. It is antichristian, as it destroys the visible unity of the body of Christ; as if he were divided against himself. It is antiscriptural, as being strictly prohibited by his sovereign authority; a direct violation of his express command. It is antinatural, as it excites Christians to contemn, to hate, and oppose one another, who are bound by the highest and most endearing obligations to love each other as brethren, even as Christ has loved them. In a word, it is productive of confusion and of every evil work.[1]

If our own movement had held true to principles such as these, there would have been a far better outcome than history has witnessed. Not only would unity in the truth have been the experience of Campbell's heirs but such a unity modeled

> *It's hard enough resisting the real enemy. That's a full-time job. If we start fighting other Christians we're fighting two wars—and one of them is suicidal.*
>
> –John Richard Wimber

by them also could have set a healthy precedent for others to imitate. As things stand, nobody could reasonably take their experience as anything but a mockery of unity in Christ.

Although there is no particular comfort in the observation, it should immediately be said that the narrowness, legalism, and propensity for division found in our movement abounds within all Christian groups. While reflections on what I have labeled "religious tribalism" and the spirit of division can be multiplied,[2] take Philip Yancey's description of his experience as a single case in point.

Surviving the Church

In the first chapter of his book *Soul Survivor*, Yancey describes an experience with which many can identify.

Sometimes in a waiting room or on an airplane I strike up conversations with strangers, during the course of which they learn that I write books on spiritual themes. Eyebrows arch, barriers spring up, and often I hear yet another horror story about the church. My seatmates must expect me to defend the church, because they always act surprised when I respond, "Oh, it's even worse than that. Let me tell you my story." I have spent most of my life in recovery from the church.[3]

Soul Survivor has an interesting subtitle: *How My Faith Survived the Church.* The church was a threat to his faith? It placed his relationship to God in jeopardy? Yancey's frustration with the church of his earlier experience parallels my own. Sadly enough, I can give you the names of people whose faith did not survive their toxic experiences with the church.

Yancey tells how he attended a 200-member church in his formative years that "had a corner on the truth, God's truth, and everyone who disagreed with us was surely teetering on the edge of hell." At the same time, though, the pastor was preaching a none-too-subtle racism from that church's pulpit. Explaining the so-called "curse of Ham" from Genesis, he told how the darker races were destined to dismal fates by the will of God. Then Yancey went away to a Bible college that had a student behavior code that ran to sixty-six pages—with creatively associated Bible passages to support them.

John and I have lived versions of Yancey's story. So have countless other persons who have trusted us with stories of their disappointment, anger, and grief that are rooted in similar experiences. Some of those people tell their stories as present-day outsiders to the church. They tell their stories to explain—perhaps boast—that they have given up on church and haven't "darkened the door" for this or that number of years. Others tell their stories with what might best be described as resignation. They are still around the edges of church—maybe, they will explain, for the sake of their children—but have no positive feelings toward it or joy in their experience of it.

Christ's "Leprous Bride"

One thing seems sure: Anyone who plans on having a relationship with Jesus Christ will have to come to terms with the church. And he or she will have to come to terms with the church in her harsh reality rather than as an idealistic dream—just as people who get married have to transition from marriage as merely a noble ideal to marriage as dirty dishes and clothes, grass that will not stay mowed, and children with runny noses.

Perhaps there is value here to the retelling of the old story of Ronald Knox's conversion to Catholicism from Anglicanism in 1917. Shortly after that event, he met an old Anglican friend who said, "Morning, Ronnie. You're looking very pleased with yourself today." "And why shouldn't I?" came the reply. "I've just become a member of the true church." "And what does it feel like to be a 'member of the true church'?" continued his friend. "Well," said Knox, "I know now, beyond a peradventure, that I am a member of the same church as Judas Iscariot."

Knox's insight is profound for those of us who struggle with the church in its flawedness. It is both natural and satisfying to think of the church as Peter and Paul, Dorcas and Prisca, Barnabas and Timothy. So conceived, the church is indeed a "radiant bride" ready to be presented to her adoring bridegroom. But the lived reality of the church is not always like that. I am also a member of that continuum of Jesus' disciples that includes Judas Iscariot, Hymanaeus and Philetus,[4] Demas,[5] and Diotrephes[6] as faithless persons who variously discredited the gospel message before a watching world. And Judas is not always present in someone else; he is sometimes in our own behavior that betrays the Holy Lord

Jesus. Or perhaps he is in the behavior of the congregation where we enjoy not only affiliation but frequent affirmation; Judas is sometimes in our behavior that devastates the spiritual life of a person or family because of our distracted inattention or ineptitude in trying to minister to them.

The gospel message does not easily permit abstraction and vagueness. We do not "embrace holiness" or "pursue authentic personhood for our spiritual lives." *We believe in Jesus of Nazareth and commit our whole beings to follow him in thought, lifestyle, and relationships with one another.* The world cannot hear and will not accept for itself a faith that is supposed to transform, stabilize, and unify Christ's followers without some concrete evidence that the church makes a difference and really matters. *The gospel is made believable by the life of a healthy community of Christ's disciples; it is discredited and made less palatable by the sorry exhibition of unprincipled behavior, anxiety, and division among people claiming to follow him.* The noble ideal for personal and corporate faith must be made concrete in the space-time world.

> *To live in love with saints above,*
> *Why that will be such glory.*
> *To dwell below with saints I know—*
> *Well, that's a different story.*
>
> –Anonymous

Someone once said, "I could believe in Christ if he did not drag behind him his leprous bride, the Church."[7] Ah, yes! That is the obstacle Yancey and others of us have had to surmount! Jesus appears to have married so far beneath himself that we are challenged to believe he is who he claims to be—if he can be joined to such a bride! Yancey and I had the incentive of wanting to find a justification for staying with (or returning to) the church, for we had begun life in her company. So we were willing to look carefully for her vindication. Increasing numbers of people have no such incentive or motivation.

But I do love the church. In spite of all the faults I know in her, she is still the bride of Christ. In spite of all the times and places where she has failed me, I have failed her far more often—and have been nurtured to health from some terrible and life-threatening crises by her. She did, after all, give me my introduction to Jesus. And she gave me occasional insights into the one thing that both justifies her existence and redeems her good name—relationships that make life holy.

Both John and I have devoted a great deal of our adult lives not only to getting over some early bad experiences of church but to trying to help at least one congregation of its people find a healthier way of "doing church" that will let Christ's bride be seen for her true beauty. In particular, we have been distressed over the sectarian posturing of the church that has made it hateful in the eyes of so many. Sectarianism spoils relationships and makes a lie of the holy vision of the church found in the pages of Scripture.

But I may have just used words that need precise definitions before going further. What does it mean to be "sectarian"? And what is "sectarianism"?

A *sectarian* is one who values his ideas, his conclusions on hard subjects, and/or his group of like-minded souls more than the truth. A sectarian is not simply someone with an opinion or point of view. He is the man who will not hear anything that challenges it. She is the woman who is so prejudiced in her belief that she refuses to face honest questions that surface in her own mind and assiduously avoids those who might call it into question. In a diverse culture, this person is a bigoted racist. In politics, he is a blind party loyalist. In religious terms, he is a sectarian. The antithesis to a sectarian is a person who is willing to follow the truth wherever it leads.

Sectarianism is a posture in things religious that defines Christian faith and practice by one's distinctive interpretations of Scripture. It is a refusal to allow for honest diversity in others and a demand for all-or-nothing conformity with her view as having exclusive approval from God. It is the minimizing or excluding of other Christians and judging that I or my group has a corner on the market of biblical truth. In toxic families, it is tyrannical dominance by one personality to whom all others must cater. In unwholesome work environments, it is an emotionally and/or physically abusive workplace where no one dares challenge a foreman or boss. The antithesis to sectarianism is respect for the intelligence and integrity of others, coupled with their loving acceptance as fellow pilgrims on an exciting spiritual journey.

Denominations vs. Sectarianism

In much of the literature and thought characteristic of writers from Churches of Christ, no distinction is made between denominationalism and sectarianism. But denominations are not sinful *per se*. More than that, they are surely inevitable and potentially valuable.

Some degree of disagreement and breaking up into diverse groups is inevitable in a fallen world populated with imperfect people. We humans are marvelously different in temperament, outlook, and taste. The two of us can write a book together but don't always like the same writers—not even the same type of literature. We disagree about some important political issues. On the other hand, some people we like least see some thorny issues the same way we do. And thinking about that too long is downright scary.

Because diversity is both real and healthy, intelligent and decent people pursue different dreams. They join different political parties. They read some biblical texts differently and are members of different denominations. These differences of view are in fact what created denominationalism. But there is nothing inherently sinful about varieties of understanding, taste, and practice that create different denominations; just look at the variations within any denomination that we seem to be able to tolerate. Sin enters this picture when one or more of them isolates itself from the others, passes judgment on their "inferior" expressions of the faith, and/or celebrates itself as the superior—perhaps even as the *only faithful*—instantiation of Christianity. What has failed in such a case is not the existence of institutional (i.e., organizational) unity but the relational unity that grows out of respect and fraternity, forbearance and love.

> *I do not want the walls of separation between different orders of Christians to be destroyed, but only lowered, that we may shake hands a little easier over them.*
>
> –Rowland Hill

Martin Luther, John Calvin, John Wesley, Alexander Campbell—these men were not in league with the devil to divide the "one church" of which the New Testament speaks but were in pursuit of Christ and attempting to renovate doctrine, polity, and practice they thought were more in keeping with heaven's ideal for the church. While these men generally counted other believers who disagreed with them as family members within the larger family of God, some of their more aggressive and less tolerant followers did not. These first-generation reformers had sought to purify faith within the larger body of Christ. Some of their second- and third-generation disciples obscured their goal. They came to have more passion for "the movement" than for the unity of Christ's spiritual body and betrayed what their forebears had envisioned.

Early Protestant theologians, Anabaptist reformers, American Restoration Movement leaders—all these figures had a concept of "catholicity" that often was lacking in some of their more ardent followers. The notion of true catholicity positively affirms those who hold the central tenets of historic Christian faith but who believe, teach, and practice differently on other matters. It is not that these "other matters" are unimportant either. These "issues" may become distinctive beliefs of a given community. They may be so important to some that they cannot teach or practice otherwise. Yet a Christian who understands and values the catholicity of the church refuses to sit in judgment on other Christ-confessors who understand church polity, the Lord's Supper, baptism, or worship differently.

Cultural Underpinnings for Denominationalism

Although every generation wants to think otherwise, each is colored by the intellectual moorings and other cultural baggage it has inherited. The Enlightenment paradigm that has served us well in many ways (e.g., medicine, space exploration, etc.) has also had its negative influences. Specifically, the dominant paradigm for rational thought for modern people has been the scientific method. With a strong confidence that human reason could fathom the depths of all things, moderns set about to study, understand, and control their environment.

The only things subject to the scientific method are, of course, physical things. So issues that could not be defined empirically didn't really matter. A.J. Ayer and the logical positivists declared that any affirmation that could not be falsified by some physical criterion that could be specified was nonsensical. So all moral statements were vacuous. Metaphysical claims about God's existence and nature were meaningless. Modernity[8] marched toward the inevitable announcement that "God is dead!" and that man has become his own savior. It was not an accident that it happened. It was the necessary outcome of the spirit of Modernity. What Robert Bellah dubbed "radical individualism" not only accounted for the drug-intoxicated, sex-saturated culture of the 1960s where each individual defined her own truth and meaning but also the theological categories that evolved during the same period.

The church was so thoroughly infected with Modernity that denominations proliferated at an astounding rate in the latter half of the twentieth century. And many of those new or offshoot denominations (e.g., the International Church of Christ, formerly known as the Boston Church of Christ and earlier as the Crossroads Movement) were sectarian to the point of being cultish. Like venerated scientists in their white coats, they reduced complex theology to simplistic formulas. Those human formulas were in turn regarded as definitions of truth. The "scientific theologians" needed and wanted no one but themselves. And they were confident that God felt just as they did!

> *What matters in the Church is not religion but the form of Christ, and its taking form amidst a band of men.*
>
> –Dietrich Bonhoeffer

Strangely enough, though, churches that sprang from and depended on the Modernist paradigm of thought contained within themselves the seeds of their own destruction. When a person's "radical individualism" was called into question by the community of faith, he or she simply bolted from the group. Personal autonomy was more important than communal participation. One writer put it this way:

> One of the striking features of much of evangelicalism is its general disregard for the institutional church. Except at the congregational level, the organized church plays a relatively minor role in the movement. Even the local congregation, while extremely important for fellowship purposes, is often regarded as a convenience to the individual. Ultimately, individuals are sovereign and can join or leave churches as they please.[9]

Since sometime in the 1980s, we have recognized a cultural shift that is obvious though still undefined in all its particulars.

For the lack of a better name, we have simply called it Post-Modernity (i.e., after-Modernity). Science's hope for discovering the predictable mechanisms of nature that would put humankind in control of all things has given way to humility and opened the door to mystery again. It is not formulas but relationships that matter—from subatomic particles to human lives! The shift is noticeably away from individualism to community. The very term "community" has become something of a buzzword in our time, and everyone can be heard affirming that we are social beings who can thrive only in healthy social networks. Might this be a time for the church to reassert its healthy presence and purpose? What do you think the impact would be in your community of a church living in the power of the Holy Spirit? Exhibiting transformed lives? Making a difference in the world?

> The kind of Christianity that attracts the new generation of Christians and will speak effectively to a postmodern world is one that emphasizes primary truths and authentic embodiment. The new generation is more interested in broad strokes than detail, more attracted to an inclusive view of the faith than an exclusive view, more concerned with unity than diversity, more open to a dynamic, growing faith than to a static fixed system, and more visual than verbal with a high level of tolerance and ambiguity.
>
> It is at these points that the link between the ancient tradition and the new generation can be made. The early tradition of the faith dealt with basic issues, and was concerned with unity, open and dynamic, mystical, relational, visual, and tangible.[10]

Are there features of Postmodernity that create concerns among people with a biblical worldview? Of course. Most versions of thought calling themselves Postmodern are highly relativistic and would resist both the exclusive claims of Jesus and the authority of Scripture. Might its penchant for mystery open people not to the Holy Spirit but to exploitive and manipulative charlatans? Certainly. *But a Postmodern world is much more like the one into which Christianity was born than the one of fifty years ago.* And that encourages us to believe the gospel can connect with people in our place and time.

Notes

1. Thomas Campbell, *Declaration and Address* (St. Louis: Mission Messenger, 1972), pp.44-47.

2. One of the funniest and most revealing of these is Garrison Keillor, *Lake Wobegon Days* (New York: Viking Penguin Inc., 1985), pp.105-106, where he tells in fictional form of the restorationist background he inherited from the Plymouth Brethren among whom he was reared. "Scholarly to the core and perfect literalists every one, they set to arguing over points that, to any outsider, would have seemed very minor indeed but which to them were crucial to the Faith.... Once having tasted the pleasure of being Correct and defending True Doctrine, they kept right on and broke up at every opportunity, until, by the time I came along, there were dozens of tiny Brethren groups, none of which were speaking to any of the others...."

3. Philip Yancey, *Soul Survivor: How My Faith Survived the Church* (New York: Doubleday, 2001), p.1.

4. Cf. 2 Timothy 2:14-26 where these two men are said to have "swerved from the truth" and are accused of "upsetting the faith of some."

5. Cf. 2 Timothy 4:10 where this brother who once served faithfully with Paul (Col. 4:14) had now "deserted" him because he was "in love with this present world."

6. Cf. 3 John 9b where John described him as a man "who likes to put himself first" and who refused to acknowledge apostolic authority.

7. Variously attributed to Percy Bysshe Shelley, Charles Algernon Swinburne, Robert Southey, et al. Perhaps the sentiment is widespread enough that such a complaint is common enough that the words can be thought of as coming from a variety of sensitive souls.

8. As a convention intended to eliminate confusion, this book speaks of "modernity" or "the spirit of modernity" instead of using the term modernism. In theological contexts, "modernism" more often signifies "liberalism" or a low view of Scripture. In broader intellectual frameworks, terms such as modernism and postmodernism have no definitional implications for a high or low view of Scripture, belief or disbelief in so cardinal a doctrine as the bodily resurrection of Jesus, etc. Readers are asked to keep this convention in minds as they proceed.

9. George F. Marsden, *Understanding Fundamentalism and Evangelicalism* (Grand Rapids: Eerdmans, 1991), p.81.

10. Robert E. Webber, *Ancient-Future Faith: Rethinking Evangelicalism for a Postmodern World* (Grand Rapids: Baker, 1999), p. 27.

True Christianity is a transcendent commitment. It cannot be achieved through our own desire to live right, to be good people, or to share what we have with others. It is not going to church or being baptized. Membership in a church organization or a religious denomination is not enough. The personal relationship with Christ is the only core around which religious life can exist.

–President Jimmy Carter

5. The Jesus Proposal / Part 2

Rubel Shelly

The original Church of God that had such an impact on its world didn't look very much like what we reference with the word "church." It certainly was not a building or geographical location—although a church will need a designated place for assembly. And it was nothing that would have been thought of as an institution in those early days—although it would ultimately need certain institutional fundamentals of leadership and organization. Neither was it what we would think of as a denomination or series of denominations—although it would not exist for long before significant steps toward dividing into distinct groups within the larger church became evident.

In its earliest days, the church was nothing more nor less than those people who had come to believe that Jesus of Nazareth was divine, the long-awaited Messiah, the Son of God, the Redeemer of Humankind. The earliest confession of these people was a simple "Jesus is Lord!" This simple confession gave them not only a sense of connection to God through Jesus but to one another. As they gathered, prayed, deepened their understanding of their confession, challenged each other to live a life worthy of their confession, and suffered, they were the church.

Even a cursory reading of the New Testament makes it clear that these groups were not uniform in organization, spiritual giftedness, understanding of Christ's return, baptismal doctrines, or the lifestyle appropriate to a Christian (i.e., Christ-follower). Thus we are likely to mis-hear a greeting such as this one: "To the church of God that is in Corinth, to those who are sanctified in Christ Jesus, called to be saints, together with all those who in every place call on the name of our Lord Jesus Christ, both their Lord and ours..." (1 Cor. 1:2).

The "church of God that is in Corinth" was not the "Church of God" of today's Bible Belt—to the exclusion of the Nazarene Church or Fourth Avenue Community Church. Specifically, this Pauline epistle was for a community of Christ-followers in an identifiable geographical region. More generally still, it would also be of value to "all those who in every place call on the name of our Lord Jesus Christ, both their Lord and ours."

The language of this text introduces us to one of the meanings of "church" in the New Testament. Not only at Corinth but in Jerusalem (Acts 8:1; 11:22), Antioch (Acts 13:1), and Ephesus (Acts 20:17), there were identifiable communities of people who confessed Christ as the Lord. Paul even wrote an epistle to "the churches of Galatia" (Gal. 1:2), a Roman province that would have included cities in Galatia such as Antioch of Pisidia, Iconium, Lystra, and Derbe (cf. Acts 13-14). Even so, we typically do not read our modern notion of denominations into the Galatian region but think of localized and interconnected groups of Christians. This is the language of what we generally label "the local church." A local church or group of local churches might, for example, gather funds in their assemblies to help other believers in distress (2 Cor. 8:1-9:15; cf. Rom. 15:25-27).

Our best evidence is that these local churches were "house churches." The church at Jerusalem began with 3,000 souls that soon became 5,000—and continued to grow quite rapidly. Although "they spent much time together in the temple" (Acts 2:46a), there was no space in the temple compound to hold regular assemblies of 3,000, 5,000, or 7,500 people. And would the Jewish authorities have permitted assemblies even approaching such numbers? So Luke informs us that the *large* local church at Jerusalem met most frequently in *small* house churches. "They broke bread at home and ate their food with glad and generous hearts, praising God and having the goodwill of all the people. And day by day the Lord added to their number those who were being saved" (Acts 2:46b-47).

> *The Church of Christ is not an institution, it is a new life with Christ and in Christ, guided by the Holy Spirit.*
>
> –Sergei Bulgakov

As the church spread and grew throughout both the Jewish territories and the larger Roman Empire, "the church" was that entire sum of individuals who met in house churches and constituted local churches (i.e., city churches) scattered everywhere. Thus *individual believers* such as Prisca and Aquila hosted a *house church* in their residence and were both individually and with their small group part of the *local church* that was the church in Rome (Rom. 16:3-5a; cf. 1 Cor. 16:19 where the same two co-workers with Paul had a "church in their house" at Ephesus).[1]

So how did the development of church organization with elder-shepherd and the ministry of deacons fit within this picture? No one can say with certainty. But since elders or bishops or pastors—interchangeable terms in the New Testament—are related to cities rather than to households (cf. Acts 20:17; Tit. 1:5), it seems more likely that they were overseers of the church in specified geographical regions rather than a given house church.[2]

There still remains the fact, of course, that the church is spoken of in a third way in the New Testament. From Jesus' promise to build "my church" (Matt. 16:18) and the references to "the church" that clearly embrace all Christians at all places at all times, we speak not only of house churches and local churches but of the universal church over which Christ functions as head to body. Nobody would think Paul was writing of either a house church or city church when he wrote this: "[God] has put all things under his feet and has made him the head over all things for the church, which is his body, the fullness of him who fills all in all" (Eph. 1:22-23).[3]

The more significant point from this usage is that the local church made up of its several house churches and many individuals was nevertheless one (universal) church rather than a network of denominations. So how does this biblical picture of individual believers, house churches, and local churches fit our modern reality? I'm not sure it does. I'm not sure it can. Neither am I sure it should.

If we genuinely believe the presence of the Holy Spirit makes the church "God's temple" (1 Cor. 3:16-17), surely it does not stretch our faith too far to affirm that he is able to preserve, expand, and adapt the church to different historical situations across time. Of course, one ahistorical view of being or restoring the church envisions "wiping the slate clean" and starting over. But not really. The group proposing to eliminate everything since Pentecost Day of Acts 2 is hardly willing to dissolve itself. And its proposal for a clean beginning is a thinly veiled sectarianism that offers: "When *you* dissolve, dismember, and cease to function and then adopt *our* beliefs, structures, and practices, God will be honored in his one true church."

Can there be unity only when there is uniformity? Or is there evidence that the Holy Spirit not only honors but creates diversity in the body? Is it possible that the Spirit of God can work with denominations today very much as he did with local churches or city churches in the first century? In a world so densely populated and gathered in cities of multiple millions, is the structural simplicity of the Mediterranean world of the first century a possibility? Was the unity of the one church ever really structural so much as relational? If the latter, can we not envision relational unity among Christian denominations so long as we avoid sectarianism? And could such relational unity not be healthy rather than detrimental to the life of the body of Christ?

Two Competing Models of the Church

Two models for the church may be called the *institutional model* and the *relational model*. While people today most naturally think in the former, I am convinced that the New Testament envisions the latter. Institutional unity thinks more in terms of structures, doctrinal formulations, exclusion of diversity, and external connections; relational unity emphasizes persons, love, inclusion of various points of view, and internal harmony. The former is church as presently experienced with its emphasis on separation rooted in distinctive beliefs and practices; the latter is the Jesus proposal which pleads for unity that affirms common beliefs and ministries.

The institutional model looks something like this:

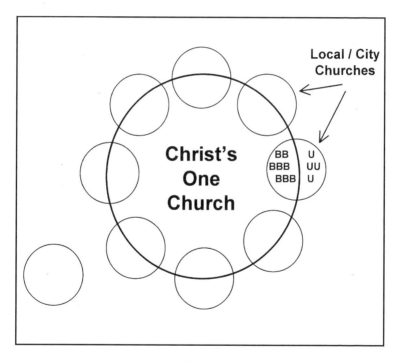

Figure 5.1

In Figure 5.1, the large circle represents the universal church, and the smaller circles represent local churches in the New Testament literature.

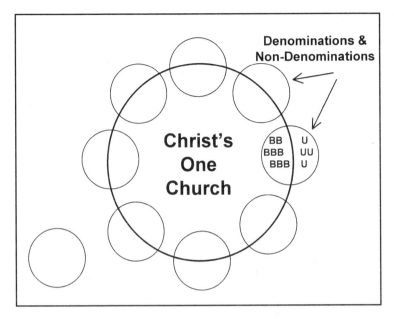

Figure 5.2

In a slight variant, Figure 5.2 still has the large circle standing for the universal church, with the small ones corresponding to denominations in our modern context. Some of these may be affiliated groups and others may be totally autonomous.

In both these depictions, please notice that each smaller circle is bisected by the larger one. This represents the fact that there actually may be unbelievers on church or denominational rosters, as well as those who are authentic believers. One should also pay attention to the occasional circle that falls completely outside the larger circle of the universal church. These represent heretical groups that make no orthodox confession about Jesus. They disavow his deity or role as Savior.

The model envisioned through these circles isn't flawless for representing a mindset, but it communicates the most common understanding of how the ancient city church or modern association of believers relates to the church Christ promised to build. Variants of it can be found in a variety of books and presentations that offer Modernity's paradigm both for interpreting the New Testament and representing the current situation built upon that understanding.[4] *But the model is ill-conceived and wrong.*

> *The Church is nothing but a section of humanity in which Christ has really taken form.*
>
> –Dietrich Bonhoeffer

For one thing, no one is acceptable to God because of his or her affiliation with a group of believers but by virtue of authentic (i.e., living, submissive, obedient) faith in Jesus Christ. Salvation is personal between the individual and her or his Lord. Though personal, salvation is not private. So each person saved by personal faith in Jesus is added to the church universal. As from the beginning of the church on Pentecost, the Lord continues to add to his universal church those who are being saved. But Christian baptism as a rite of initiation is not to be understood as one's entrance into local church membership so much as "into Christ"—his spiritual body, his universal church. "As many of you as were baptized into Christ have clothed ourselves with Christ" (Gal. 3:28).[5]

If the paragraph above is correct, the model with bisected and excluded circles is mistaken. We are drawn to it for its neatness in allowing each of us to see not only herself but others in relation to the institution. It provides neat boundary markers for the beliefs or behaviors that separate insiders from outsiders. But this sounds suspiciously like the exercise of human power in the name of religion.

A relational model for being the church would look more like this:

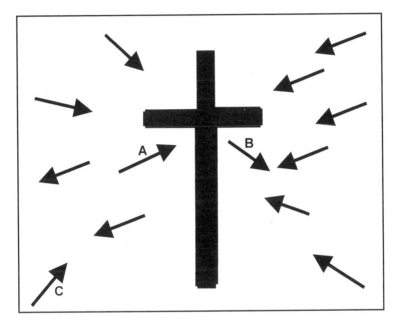

Figure 5.3

This model foregoes the "neatness" of circles for the sake of a central person, Jesus Christ. It does not have the sharp lines of exclusion visible anywhere. Instead, it has arrows pointing toward or away from Christ. The status of a distant arrow moving toward him would be more desirable than that of a close one moving out from his presence.

Translated into specifics, Person C who is distant from Christ by virtue of greed, racism, or promiscuity but who is now being drawn to him in dawning faith and/or early penitence has greater hope of being accepted for salvation than Person B who is a church deacon or the leader of last Sunday's opening prayer in the plenary assembly of the church but whose heart is increasingly fixed and hard in its greed, racism, or ongoing affair. If this is not true, what is the meaning of the Parable of the Pharisee and the Tax Collector (Luke 18:9-14)?

By neat circles and membership rolls, however, the Pharisee would have been the "insider" to Jesus' story. The tax collector would have been "outside" the institutional lines. Yet Jesus—who pays more attention to the heart than to externals—said it was the latter who went home justified that day. This situation did not change after Pentecost, for we still find institutional insiders binding circumcision on Gentiles, pulling power plays in local churches, and being judged anti-Christ by an apostle.

The ideal in this scenario is, of course, represented by Person A. This is a teachable and penitent believer. This is the person who will not tolerate deliberate sin in his or her life. This is the one who loves God and the righteousness to which he calls believers through Scripture. This is the one who loves others and treats them with dignity, respect, and compassion.

In his letter to the local church at Sardis, Jesus judged it apostate church and about to die. "Yet you have still a few persons in Sardis who have not soiled their clothes," Jesus said. "They will walk with me, dressed in white, for they are worthy" (Rev. 3:4). By the chart with circles and lines, the church at Sardis—and all its constituent members—was renegade to the faith. It was the church none of us would encourage members moving from our town to Sardis to join. Yet Jesus looked with favor on certain individuals in that corrupt-and-dying church.

In warning Timothy and others about false teachers and false doctrines, Paul assured him, "But God's firm foundation [i.e., the church] stands, bearing this inscription: 'The Lord knows those who are his' " (2 Tim. 2:19a). Are we willing for the Lord to know his own? Are we willing to abdicate judgment for mercy? Are we willing to be less institutional and more relational with Christ and one another? These questions are hardly rhetorical! They are at the heart of trying to be humble believers in imperfect churches for the sake of honoring Christ. They propose nothing that resembles the compromise of one's own faith; they reject the harsh judgments that have allowed sectarianism to flourish. They do not demolish denominations and their distinctives today; neither did they create uniformity in the first-century church. But they do establish a framework in which believers may exchange and debate points of view to mutual advantage. All the while, these same people are able to bear unified witness to the saving power of Jesus Christ.

An Outline of the Proposal

For the sake of clarity, *The Jesus Proposal* calls for us to model personal faith in Christian communities that display unity in the midst of their diversity. Although the intellectual framework of Modernity could hardly fathom such a paradigm, it is eminently workable for a Postmodern culture that shares more with the first century than the nineteenth or twentieth. There is an "ambiguity" about such a proposal for Moderns. They were taught to seek fixed and objective understandings for every text. Postmoderns have no difficulty with less-than-perfect interpretations, for they value persons over formulas.

1. *Spiritual fellowship begins on the foundation of confessed love for and faith in Jesus Christ.* The language of Paul comes to mind here as he addressed his letter not only to an identifiable body of baptized believers at Corinth but also to "all those who in every place call on the name of our Lord Jesus Christ, both their Lord and ours: Grace to you and peace from God our Father and the Lord Jesus Christ" (1 Cor. 1:2b-3). The tendency of institutional churches is to begrudge the inclusion of others into their organization—to put their names on a roll, to account them as members, to judge them worthy of participation in the fellowship of the group. Think about it. Does that seem consistent with Jesus' personal model? Did he incline to *ex*-clusion (i.e., prohibiting participation) or *in*-clusion (i.e., inviting people to his fellowship upon minimal conditions)?

> *The church is not a gallery for the exhibition of eminent Christians, but a school for the education of imperfect ones.*
>
> –Henry Ward Beecher

In most cases, churches operating from an institutional mindset wait for some level of application for membership before admitting candidates to anything more than the public events of the church. Thus the Lord's Supper would be discouraged—if not prohibited—for the unbaptized in practically every church setting.[6] This does not honor the example of Jesus. He took the initiative with all people who showed goodwill toward him and shared the fellowship experience of sitting at table with them. "This fellow welcomes sinners and eats with them" was meant as an insult to Jesus' orthodoxy by the Pharisees and scribes (Luke 15:2). Fortunately for us, the very same statement is the assurance of his gracious welcome upon minimal conditions. Just as Alcoholics Anonymous has as its condition of membership the acknowledgment of addiction to alcohol and the desire for sobriety—but not the attainment of it—a relational church needs nothing more than openness to Christ's message to welcome people to its table or to join its spiritual journey.

> [T]he church as a community invites all who would seek God through Jesus to the table. It invites the sinner, the unchurched and the weak family member to the table to hear the gospel of grace. It invites all to learn the gospel through eating and drinking. It should invite all except the disciplined who have demonstrated their disdain for the table through their rebellious lifestyle.[7]

2. *A local church is the nurturing spiritual community within which one may learn, be initiated into, and begin living the basic teachings that establish and declare one's identity as a Christian (i.e., Christ-follower).*

It seems impossible for the universal church to be my sphere of acquaintance, education, and ministry—in any meaningful way.[8] For the sake of day-to-day belonging and support, regular instruction in the faith, Lord's Day worship, and the like, each of us needs a church that has a name and local address. While you may fill out a survey form about religious affiliation by checking "Christian," you invite your new neighbor to attend a Sunday service with you at a church that can be located on a city map. While one of us might begin a conversation with a Muslim friend about Christianity "in general," any perceived interest on his part will soon lead us to define Christianity "in particular" in terms of a heritage in the Church of Christ, Pentecostal Church, Greek Orthodox Church, or some other tradition.

Here we run into the problem again of the difference in cultures between first and twenty-first centuries. In the first century, Paul could have encouraged someone he led to faith in Christ while under house arrest at Rome to look up "the believers" or "his new brothers and sisters" when he returned to his home in Philippi or Thessalonica. The issue of which denomination or sub-set of Christians to contact in that city would not have come up—not, at least, in the earliest days of the church.[9]

In the twenty-first century, it is unlikely that anyone gets acquainted with generic Christian faith. Her Presbyterian friend in the carpool began sharing the story of Christ with her and colored it with Presbyterian language, forms, and distinctive interpretations. If, on the other hand, she began her journey toward Jesus in the context of a marriage that was falling apart and a clerk inviting her tearful customer to a revival service at a Baptist Church, she will hear the story of Jesus with a slant and vocabulary different from that of Presbyterians.

I spoke above of the gospel being "colored" by its presentation from a certain perspective. Each of us colors whatever story he or she tells by virtue of background, culture, unique perspectives, and studied conclusions. But coloring need not be equated with "perverting" or "misrepresenting" the story. More often than not in the era of Modernity and its vaunted search for "objectivity," teachers were inclined to an

all-or-nothing approach to their points of view. One's per-
ception of the millennium, church organization, or present-
day activity of the Holy Spirit would more nearly wind up as
his "test of fellowship" than the core gospel. Such an
approach is positively unbiblical, as attested by Paul's counsel in Romans 14.

The essence of Romans 14 is not to tell disputing brothers that their issues are unimportant. Neither is it to give the
definitive apostolic answer to them. Come to think of it, the
Enlightenment paradigm that has dominated Christian
thought for the past two centuries would have all but
required one or the other of these approaches. Irrevocable
answers and a mechanism for enforcing their acceptance is a
method we know all too well. Instead, Paul dealt with the
doctrinal disputes in the city church of Rome relationally
instead of institutionally. "Let all be fully convinced in their
own minds.... Let us therefore no longer pass judgment on
one another, but resolve instead never to put a stumbling
block or hindrance in the way of another" (Rom. 14:5b,13).

So long as the core gospel message of sin and salvation,
of our inadequacy and Christ's sufficiency, is taught, can we
not apply Paul's counsel to our discussions of ecclesiology,
eschatology, and pneumatology? So long as repentance and
faith in Christ as Savior is proclaimed as gospel, can we not
grant that intelligent people of goodwill may come to contrary conclusions about nuances of baptismal theology?
Although every item of Christian theology is important, not
every item is equally important. The gospel defined as the
redemptive death, burial, and resurrection of Jesus for sinners
is "of first importance" to a biblical theology (1 Cor. 15:1-4).
But this is the fundamental message passed on by those who

take Scripture seriously in all Christian denominations. If a friend from work who is an atheist or a Hindu knows anything about his Charismatic, Methodist, or Roman Catholic neighbor, it almost certainly will be this much.

What varies among these denominations is less the definition of the gospel than their specification of the faith-response appropriate to the gospel. Those who affirm immersion as the more ancient and theologically expressive *mode* of baptism do not always agree on the *immediacy* or *necessity* to attach to it. If we clear these hurdles, we may still bump into the thorny issue of the relationship of water baptism to Holy Spirit baptism or a variety of other related topics.

Do such differences of interpretation and practice matter? Surely they do! So long as the gospel is preached, however, are we not obliged to honor and affirm any person or group offering it to unbelievers? So long as one does not err into the extreme opposite positions of baptismal regeneration, on one hand, or a faith that is mere intellectual assent apart from personal surrender to Christ on the other, does not even the New Testament reveal a variety of examples on baptismal experience? After hearing the gospel, the Ethiopian (Acts 8:36) and a jailer at Philippi (Acts 16:33) were baptized without delay. Saul of Tarsus was baptized several days after his encounter with the Risen Christ on the Damascus Road (Acts 9:9,17-19). And a Roman centurion named Cornelius appears to have been baptized in the Holy Spirit well before he heard anything about water baptism (Acts 10:44-48).

I don't know what to make of the lack of strict uniformity in these conversion events in the New Testament—except that God is not bound to a pattern that has him doing things with uniformity, that God is more concerned with relationship than with regularity. The mindset of Modernity makes us search for the regularity typical of our scientific models. Some of us have forced the non-uniform examples of conversion into a homogeneous and standardized formula. Even on the paradigm of modern science, however, we should have been intelligent enough to see that, just as scientific laws are descriptive rather than prescriptive, so the cases of conversion in Acts are descriptive of anecdotal events rather than prescriptive of any one model. If there was a series of "fixed and inflexible steps" to salvation—whether three, five, seven, or seventy-seven steps—they could have been listed somewhere in systematic fashion. But that was neither the method of God nor the mindset of the biblical writers.

> *Biblically the church is an organism not an organization—a movement, not a monument. It is not a part of the community, it is a whole new community. It is not an orderly gathering; it is a new order with new values.*
>
> –Charles W. Colson

Our attempts to find—or, more correctly, *force*—a biblical pattern onto anecdotal evidence has made line-drawing exclusions by theologians operating with a certain mindset inevitable. It does not lapse into relativism to grant that there is some ambiguity in the biblical case studies. To the contrary, it says that Christ and his messengers met people where they were in their diverse spiritual quests. Only a rigid institutional model would require giving each one a formula identical to that presented to every other. It appears that the only identical item in the various settings and with diverse life situations was Jesus, a person rather than a policy. This means that something relational rather than institutional was the means to the conversion of the individuals and the creation of a subsequent relationship among them.

3. Unity with the larger body of Christ is evidenced and maintained in a lifestyle that honors the Son of God.

If the initial education and nurturing a neophyte believer needs comes through a local church or denomination, how does that same believer witness to his or her connection to the church universal? Since the beliefs and practices of churches vary in some significant particulars, how can an individual within one of those bodies share in what used to be termed the "catholicity" of the church?[10] The universal witness Christians of whatever locale, denomination, or function in the church bear to their commitment to Christ and love for his people is holiness.

The fruit of the Spirit—love, joy, peace, patience, kindness, generosity, faithfulness, gentleness, and self-control (Gal. 5:22-23)—testifies not only to the authenticity of an individual believer's faith but to her participation in the body of Christ. This link between the Holy Spirit and lifestyle is a major theme of 1 Corinthians. Paul insists that both the corporate church (1 Cor. 3:16) and the individual's believer's body (1 Cor. 6:19) are temples for the Holy Spirit. The point is not that the Holy Spirit has two residences, but one. All those who have been regenerated by the Holy Spirit (cf. Tit. 3:5) live in, are inhabited by, and receive empowerment from the Spirit of God.

One of the Corinthian issues Paul addressed in a variety of ways was oneness amidst their diversity, unity transcending difference. For one thing, there were rival loyalties to evangelists and leaders known to the church at Corinth. "For when one of you says, 'I belong to Paul,' and another, 'I belong to Apollos,' are you not merely human?" he chided (1 Cor. 3:4). The extent to which these loyalties were creating conflict in the city church of Corinth is clear from Paul's strong language about their still being "of the flesh" and "behaving according to human inclinations" (1 Cor. 3:3). A small part of the solution to that problem was to realize that Paul and Apollos, for example, were not competitors in ministry but servants to Christ, fellow-laborers, and men of "common purpose" (1 Cor. 3:5-16).

But far more significant than the attitude of two evangelists toward each other was the fact that Spirit-presence is expressly designed to produce a spiritual holiness that surpasses the flesh and normal human inclinations. "Do you not know that you are God's temple and that God's Spirit dwells in you?" asked Paul. "If anyone destroys God's temple, God will destroy that person. For God's temple is holy, and you are that temple" (1 Cor. 3:16-17).

Another problem in the same local church had to do with a diversity of spiritual gifts among its members. Apparently those with "flashier" gifts such as tongues-speaking felt superior and communicated their feelings in a variety of ways. The apostle's response to the rifts that had grown out of these sentiments were pragmatic in part. For example, he envisioned an unbeliever coming into an assembly where several were speaking in tongues and being turned off to the whole Christian enterprise as an exercise in insanity. "If, therefore, the whole church comes together and all speak in tongues, and outsiders or unbelievers enter, will they not say that you are out of your mind?" (1 Cor. 14:23).

Again, however, Paul's weightier answer to the Corinthian problem was not an appeal either to image or impact but for the believers in that city to understand why the Holy Spirit was active among them at all. "For just as the body is one and has many members, and all the members of the body, though many, are one body, so it is with Christ. For in one Spirit we were all baptized into one body—Jews or Greeks, slaves or free—and we were all made to drink of one Spirit" (1 Cor. 12:12-13).

Self-promotion, rivalries in ministry, sexual perversions, corruption of the Lord's Supper—these and a variety of other problems that were hindering the church at Corinth betrayed a lack of maturity among Christians there. These unattractive and sinful behaviors were spoiling the church's witness to the larger community. Only if the church renewed its allegiance to Christ by allowing the Spirit to produce a lifestyle among them that honored the One they confessed as their Redeemer could it maintain its relationship to the larger body of Christ.

> *It would scarcely be necessary to expound doctrine if our lives were radiant enough. If we behaved like true Christians, there would be no pagans.*
>
> –Pope John XXIII

This reading of the Corinthian correspondence is altogether consistent with what the same apostle wrote in another place: "I therefore, the prisoner in the Lord, beg you to lead a life worthy of the calling to which you have been called, with all humility and gentleness, with patience, bearing with one another in love, making every effort to maintain the unity of the Spirit in the bond of peace" (Eph. 4:1-3). Notice first from this text that unity is not a goal for the church to achieve. It is a God-given reality for the church to maintain and evidence to the world. The means by which this unity has been created is the Holy Spirit, and it is exhibited to the world through such unique Christian virtues as humility, gentleness, patience, and love.

4. *Oneness with Christ and his body is enhanced by means of a commitment to and pursuit of doctrinal purity within the revealed will of God in Holy Scripture.*

I can imagine the frustration of some who were trained to think as I was in following these summary points this far. The first is "far too vague, ambiguous, and subjective" in its willingness to initiate *any* form of spiritual fellowship on the basis of nothing more than love for and faith in Jesus Christ, and the second "positively abandons the commitment to doctrinal purity enjoined on Christians in the New Testament." Let me repeat: I know where that thinking comes from and would have argued the same thing myself at an earlier time in my life. Even to acknowledge that much, however, can be heard as an arrogant put-down of those who still hold a view I now consider wrong—*doctrinally* wrong. To the contrary, I affirm their desire to be good Bible students who reason carefully and search for the truth on every point of biblical revelation.

True faith in Jesus Christ typically begins as a vague, ambiguous, and subjective response to the attractiveness of his person. Is a young child of nine or eleven who confesses Christ and is baptized in his name even doctrinally literate, much less doctrinally sound? Is a novice fresh out of the dark world of moral confusion able to articulate a clear doctrine of repentance, much less five-point Calvinism? Is a man who has just returned to the mooring of his earliest childhood memory on account of the dissolution of his family to be asked, "Do you believe that Jesus Christ is the Son of God?" or "Do you subscribe to a view of symbolic or actual presence in Holy Communion?"

If individuals cannot come to Christ and be saved on such a minimum of doctrinal content that some could rightfully say they know little more than the name of the person they are confessing as their Savior, how shall we explain Pentecost of Acts 2? How shall we explain what we know about the original circulation of the New Testament documents? Could someone become a Christian with nothing more than the Gospel of Luke or John? Perhaps we forget that for only a fraction of the time since Jesus have people had access to copies of the Bible. Perhaps we forget that the vast majority of people who have lived in any given generation prior to very recent times were not able to read. Perhaps these questions and bits of general knowledge have not been factored into our conclusions about circumstances under which people did in fact learn of and bow their knees to Christ as Savior. If the New Testament teaches anything at all, it teaches that we are not saved by good works of any kind—including theological education and doctrinal precision—but by faith in Jesus Christ. Saying all this, however, is *not* to disparage doctrinal purity.

The process of Christian discipleship involves two important moves. The first is "faith," and the second is "the faith."
There is a difference between one's first subjective move
toward Jesus in loving and trusting him as Savior and the later
appreciation she will grow to have for issues such as the one
being explored in this book. One's ability to articulate an
ecclesiology (i.e., doctrine of the church) that is relational
rather than institutional is altogether unnecessary for salvation—but important in its place and time. A clearer understanding of the principles and practices of Christian worship
are incredibly valuable—but not essential for redemption from
sin. And so on with dozens of other points of doctrine that
have their place in the total process of Christian maturity.

What a difference it would have made in church history if
Christ-confessors could have studied and debated their diver-
gent understandings of Christian theology with respect for one
another as children of God. The rancor and bloodshed that are
so embarrassing in history and in newspapers might have
been avoided. The unity for which Christ prayed "so that the
world may believe that [God the Father] sent me" (John 17:21)
might have been witnessed more often. We have needed the
insights into worship of my Charismatic and Pentecostal brothers and sisters. We have needed the Wesleyan challenge to
holy living. And we might have been able to offer an occasional insight or challenge peculiar to Churches of Christ—if
we had been in loving dialogue rather than insecure rivalry.

Doctrinal issues have been disputed in the church
since the beginning, and such argument can be
healthy. When we do this unlovingly, however, we
unleash our own base instincts. We become more

strident to mask our own insecurity, and we use doc-trinal disputes as an excuse to grab power.[11]

Following his comments about Christian attitude and lifestyle already cited, Paul continued: "There is one body and one Spirit, just as you were called to the one hope of your calling, one Lord, one faith, one baptism, one God and Father of all, who is above all and through all and in all" (Eph. 4:4-6). Each of these doctrinal elements is important. Yet there is no good reason to think Paul intended it as an exhaustive list of items of value to believers or even as a min-imal creed that could serve as the basis for doctrinal unity. When we accept the fact that there is no "list" or "formula" on the basis of which we find God or claim a relationship with him, we will see far more health in the Christian com-munity. He saves us by taking the initiative for our souls. And that initiative was ultimately in a person, not by means of a recipe or blueprint. The respectful and loving study of doc-trinal differences could even help us appreciate this most fundamental fact of our common faith.

5. *Unity in Christ is demonstrated to unbelievers by acts of joint witness and ministry by individual Christians, small groups, and/or local churches.*

Earlier I referred to Paul's gathering of funds among Gentile churches for their Jewish counterparts in a time of famine. What a blessing those gifts must have been to the needy saints in and around Jerusalem! What an affirmation of the unity of Jews and Gentiles in the body of Christ. And what a witness to unbelievers when they saw such an outpouring of generosity! We can hardly doubt that such behaviors bridged longstanding ethnic divisions and turned out to be "pre-evangelistic contact" with many pagan onlookers who saw so healthy a thing and explored its origin. In doing so, they were found by Christ.

The same sort of joint witness and ministry by believers today is more powerful than our typical go-it-alone strategies of evangelism and compassion. But perhaps we are merely perpetuating a precedent from the New Testament in being so sectarian. Do you remember the day when his disciples—with no less than John as their spokesperson—told Jesus, "Teacher, we saw someone casting out demons in your name, and we tried to stop him, because he was not following us"? (Mark 9:39). The key element of the complaint is clearly that the man "was not following us"—was not a member of their group or organization. Jesus rebuked them for what they had done and challenged them to think relationally rather than institutionally. "Do not stop him; for no one who does a deed of power in my name will be able soon afterward to speak evil of me. Whoever is not against us is for us. For truly I tell you, whoever gives you a cup of water to drink because you bear the name of Christ will by no means lose the reward" (Mark 9:38-41).

> *Christianity is not a collection of truths to be believed, of laws to be obeyed. Christianity is a person. Christianity is Christ.*
>
> –Oscar Romero

Out of a background of refusal to cooperate with people from other Christian traditions (except perhaps occasionally to oppose liquor referenda, abortion clinics, or state-sponsored gambling), this event from the ministry of Jesus comes as a staggering rebuke. Its clear and manifest teaching challenges the consistent practice of my background in Churches of Christ. But what an incredible sense of joy comes from repentance.

Some of the most enriching spiritual experiences John and I had in the 1990s were at Promise Keepers events in Nashville, Memphis, Atlanta, and Washington. In particular, the Atlanta rally in February of 1996 focused on pastors and ministers of all denominations who confessed Christ as the Son of God. At a count of three, Max Lucado had the tens of thousands in the Georgia Dome to shout the name of their denomination or local church. There was an incredible din of noise from which no clear and distinct sound could be discerned. He then asked for the same audience to shout the name of the one to whom its members looked for salvation and life. The result was gloriously different as a sweet chorus exalted the name of Jesus Christ as with one voice. It was only an illustration, but a powerful and dramatic one. Relational unity with other believers is now a live option for Christians who once were willing to live with relationships ranging from benign neglect to raging opposition. We would be wise to remember the words of Jesus to his earliest disciples about trying to silence anyone bearing witness to him.

Events and ministries done jointly with others who confess Christ help us overcome our past bigotries and judgments. They also help us make a powerful statement to those who are turned off to Christianity because of its merciless sectarianism. They are able to glimpse at least the possibility that love for Christ has more power to bring his followers together than their denominational loyalties to keep them apart.

6. *The church will be seen mature and spotless as the grace-creation of Christ himself at his* parousia.

When we have done all we can to build up the local church, reach out to those who do not know Christ, and live in Spirit-given unity, we will nevertheless fall woefully short. At our best, we are limited mortals who fail not only from rebellion but from weakness, insufficiency, and ignorance. Before God's desire for his redeemed people to be one fold with one shepherd can be realized, he will have to take the initiative in one grand, final move.

The word will be given. With angels as his attending servants, Jesus will return. He will claim his own from all places, ethnic groups, skin colors, and languages. And he will finally and forever purge the residue of sin from the race. "Then comes the end, when he hands over the kingdom to God the Father, after he has destroyed every ruler and every authority and power" (1 Cor. 15:24). Until that day, what shall we do? Until the final and definitive redemption of the entire faithful church, how do we honor him in our present state of institutional division?

"What a Friend..."

Syndicated columnist Deborah Mathis wrote about a day in her life in our nation's capital.[12] She told about passing through busy Union Station. The first thing stamped on her memory was the noisy hubbub of sounds. The public address announcer calling out arrivals and departures. Scores of pagers, walkie-talkies, and cell phones crying out for someone's attention. There were horns honking, machines clinking out change, and babies crying. There were voices from every direction. A nervous security guard yelled with his best post-9/11 voice at a man about to enter a forbidden area. Three women stood up from their bench in order to press the points of their squabble with more emphasis. The man in line in front of her was pacing in tiny, agitated steps. Then she heard someone singing:

> What a friend we have in Jesus,
> All our sins and griefs to bear;
> What a privilege to carry
> Everything to God in prayer.
> O what peace we often forfeit,
> O what needless pain we bear,
> All because we do not carry
> Everything to God in prayer.

And a perceptible change came over the cacophonous crowd. The quarreling women closed down their spat and quietly took their seats. Tense shoulders seemed to relax. As the lone voice sang the remaining verses of Joseph Scriven's lyrics from 150 years ago to a tune composed by Charles C. Converse, Ms. Mathis realized she was singing along now. So were the three women who had been bickering. And several more.

> Have we trials and temptations?
> Is there trouble anywhere?
> We should never be discouraged,
> Take it to the Lord in prayer.
> Can we find a Friend so faithful,
> Who will all our sorrows share?
> Jesus knows our every weakness:
> Take it to the Lord in prayer.

"Nice, huh?" offered the man who had been pacing his tiny, tight circle in front of her. "I don't even believe in Jesus, but that's nice."

Reading about Ms. Mathis' experience, are you not touched deeply by it—perhaps because of your own experience of Jesus as the friend who stands closer than a brother? And think especially of that man who said, "I don't even believe in Jesus, but that's nice." If we distracted and disconnected, distanced and divided folks who say we love, believe in, and follow Christ could learn to practice relational unity, surely it would have an impact. People would say, "That's nice!" People who've had no use for Christianity because of its disgraceful sectarianism would see something attractive in its place. Philip Yancey-types whose souls have not managed to survive the confusion of our denominational and non-denominational teachings, who feel betrayed by our all-too-common hypocrisies such as racism and sexism, or who have been ground up in church politics just might find hope to try again—this time looking for spirituality centered on Jesus rather than religiosity rooted in convention and custom.

> Are we weak and heavy laden,
> Cumbered with a load of care?
> Precious Savior, still our refuge,
> Take it to the Lord in prayer.
> Do thy friends despise, forsake thee?
> Take it to the Lord in prayer;
> In His arms He'll take and shield thee,
> Thou wilt find a solace there.

In the power of the Holy Spirit, the church could still shift the attention of the world to Jesus. If we experience and

present Friend Jesus as Lord rather than Commandant Jesus
as Warden, Life-Transforming Jesus as Redeemer rather than
Soul-Stifling Jesus as Prude and Spoilsport, thousands—even
millions—would embrace him. Instead of being turned off by
his "leprous bride," they could be induced to come to him by
a joyous church—fairly radiant in her true catholicity.

It is a noble proposal to pray about: Maintaining the unity
of the body of Christ. It is a project only he could bring to
completion: To teach us how to be one family—alike and different, to the praise and honor of God.

Notes

1. This is a consistent phenomenon in the New Testament literature.
Philemon was a member of the city church of Colossae and hosted a house
church in his residence (Phile. 1-2). From the epistle "to the saints and faithful brothers and sisters in Christ in Colossae," we know of at least one other
of the house churches that made up the city church. Paul greeted "Nympha
and the church in her house" (Col. 4:15). This also helps us understand the
situation Paul addressed in 1 Corinthians. "Chloe's people" (NRSV) or "some
from Chloe's household" (NIV) reported to him that there was growing division among the saints at Corinth. Different house-church groups within the
local church at Corinth were apparently declaring their loyalties through
favorite teachers who had influenced them (cf. 1 Cor. 1:10-17).

2. The notion of a monarchical bishop with "apostolic succession" and
the right to hold the church together with judgments about orthodox doctrine is a second- and third-century development and not a New Testament
means to unity. This was the beginning of institutional unity over against the
relational unity found in the biblical text.

3. Cf. Ephesians 3:10, 21; 4:3-6; 5:23-32.

4. Although this model fits well with Modernity's worldview, it neither came into being with Enlightenment thinkers nor leaps from the pages of the New Testament. A doctrine of the true church as "invisible" and a "mixed multitude" developed and became dominant in the fourth century, with Augustine as a spokesman for it.

5. There are certainly other issues about baptism that are to be addressed elsewhere in this book. Is it to be performed by sprinkling or immersion? Is it prior to salvation or after? Is it a time or means of the impartation of saving grace? For now, the only issue at stake is baptism as a sign of one's entrance into Christ and his spiritual body, the church.

6. Protestant denominations have different practices about "open" versus "closed" communion. Closed communion has been the more widespread practice. In Churches of Christ, a middle-ground (and thoroughly Modernist) policy of allowing each person to make an individual decision about participation has been the general rule.

7. John Mark Hicks, *Come to the Table: Revisioning the Lord's Supper* (Orange, CA: New Leaf Books, 2002), p. 170. I recommend this book as the starting point for a careful study of the Lord's Supper as a joyous community celebration of the Risen Christ instead of a doleful and solitary time of reflection on the agonies of his death.

8. Perhaps some parachurch ministries and their fundraisers see their primary relationship with the body as coming through the universal rather than local church. But we have had to invent both the term "parachurch" to describe these ministries and a methodological framework within which they can operate. Perhaps this is why they have been so controversial at times. Perhaps this is why the most effective ones are those that both work through and affirm the ministries of local churches.

9. It is altogether possible, however, that some equivalent discussion would have to take place between John and a non-resident convert at Ephesus who was about to leave for his home in a town where he knew there was a presence of heretical disciples who were either questioning or denying outright that Jesus had come in the flesh (cf. 1 John 4:2-3).

10. In Christian literature as early as the second century, writers employed "catholicity" as a term whose clear purpose was to affirm their understanding of the church as a single body made up of all those who

belong to God through Jesus Christ. It was deemed a broad-enough term to cover all the local or city churches in whatever diverse geographical or ethnic settings they were found. That early Christians writers understood the term this way is apparent in statements such as this one: "Where the bishop is present, there let the congregation gather, just as where Jesus Christ is, there is the Catholic Church." Ignatius *To the Smyrneans* 8. 2. as translated in Baillie, John, McNeill, John T., and Van Dusen, Henry P., eds. The Library of Christian Classics. Vol. I: *Early Christian Fathers* (Philadelphia: Westminster Press, 1953), p. 115. A clearer translation would have omitted capital letters in favor of simply "catholic church," for the reference here is not to a particular denomination or sect but to the church in totality.

11. Charles W. Colson, *The Body* (Dallas: Word, 1992), p. 100.

12. Deborah Mathis, "What a friend, as the hustle goes by," *The (Nashville) Tennessean*, June 14, 2002, p. 17A.

There never was a time when church was not dialogically and dialectically related to culture, not even in the New Testament period itself that set the patterns for churches of the Apostolic and Ante-Nicene eras. . . . We cannot characterize the communities of faith that emerge in the earliest days of the church under a single, unambiguous paradigm. Christian communities were as varied as the human cultures from which they emerged.

—Michael Jinkins

6. STRENGTHS OF THE PROPOSAL

John O. York

Jesus Christ is the same, yesterday and today and forever" (Heb.13:8). Hebrews is not well-known to most of us, aside from a few one-liners like this one. The stability of Jesus Messiah in the midst of all that changes in the world around us is indeed a comforting thought.

We usually hear the verse quoted when there is talk about everything else in our world changing. Our life circumstances are so volatile, so fragile. Jobs and houses and family structures too often are not as stable as we want to think they are. One of the reasons people long for stability in church is because we long for some place, some moment, some circumstance in our lives that is stable and secure. This is the verse people quote when we want to make (or resist!) changes in worship styles.

But it is Jesus—not the songs or the order of worship or the location of the building or the times of worship—who remains the same.

Interpretations Are Not Static

Problems arise, however, when we begin to face our own diversity and particularity as individuals and communities of faith. How do we break out of the divisive spirit that has dominated church history for the past five centuries and seek, instead, to "maintain the unity of the Spirit in the bond of peace?" How do we leave behind the individualism and sectarianism that produced hair-splitting debate and begin to live out in our time the prayer of Jesus that his followers be one just as he and his Father are one? How do we stop thinking of churches as organizations and start understanding the church as organism—as the living body of Christ rather than an institution?

At the heart of what we have labeled the Jesus Proposal is the firm conviction that, while Jesus Christ is indeed the same, yesterday, today and forever, our human understandings and perceptions of Jesus are ever-changing. This, to me, is the most difficult challenge to our longings for stability and security.

There is no uniform, static understanding of God or of Jesus that can be traced through church history. What you find instead are doctrines of God and Christ and church that are shaped by the times, circumstances, and belief systems of the people who advance them. As Brian McLaren puts it, we humans tend to describe God as a better, greater version of ourselves. Thus,

> for the conservatives, God is a conservative (surprise!); for the liberals, God is liberal; for the intellectuals God is clothed in abstractions and complexities; while for the uneducated, God is a down-to-earth and

simple kind of guy. For the military man, God tends to be about power; while for the bureaucrat God is about policies. For the artist God has a wildness and beauty that inspires and attracts; while for the engineer, God's grandeur is in predictability, stability and definition—opposite qualities of those loved by the artist. For the social worker, God sides with the poor and oppressed; while for the entrepreneur, God rewards the diligent and clever.[1]

McLaren goes on to suggest that the same is true in the larger perspectives of East versus West or industrialized verse non-industrialized cultures. Of course, in the amazing story of God called Scripture, one can find a text to support any of those portrayals.

It is little wonder that the church as institution has flourished over the past 200 years in America or that church leadership and organization structures closely resemble those of the business world. Corporate structures and institutional design are the very fabric of American life. No one in American culture should be surprised that God wants to "increase our territory" and bless us with more and

> *Trusting Christ for salvation means ceasing to trust in our own efforts to be righteous.*
>
> –William Tyndale

more material wealth—or that we should find a proof-text that gives biblical sanction to our voracious desires. They are at the heart of our capitalist economic system.

Neither should anyone be surprised that evangelism became church growth, which in turn became "marketing" the church. One targets market shares and advertises appropriately in order to grow big companies and big churches. We should not be surprised that in a culture that prizes individualism and personal choice that churches cater to felt needs and individual desires.

Though we sometimes protest conforming Christian faith to our culture, how do we escape the realization that God and Christ and our interpretations of Scripture and our pursuit of faith are inevitably conditioned by our circumstances? The answer is that we *don't* and *can't* escape them. Neither can we any longer pretend that *our* faith and *our* practices in a particular church are immune or that there was a time called "Bible times" that was immune. There never has been a time when some pristine form of Christian faith lived outside of such cultural reading.

The "Conditioning" of Modernity

The search in Scripture for some sort of church pattern, when you think about it, is a culturally conditioned response to the biblical text in the new world of science and industrialization. That nineteenth- and twentieth-century search for patterns assumed a "blueprint model" for everything that was good. Draw up the business plan. Produce the architectural drawings for the house or the skyscraper. Everything has a structure that we are able to figure out. Surely God's design is there for the taking in Scripture. Thus when you even find the word "pattern" in Scripture, that must be the plan![2] So why did so many architects end up with so many different blueprints, all claiming to be the only suitable plan?

Rubel and I are proposing a different way of viewing the people of God, a different way of describing what it means to be Christian. Maybe all we are doing is drawing up yet another set of blueprints! But what I hope we're describing has mystery and rather chaotic, undrawable characteristics. We dubbed it a *relational* model as opposed to an *institutional* model. We've begun to describe a way of reading Scripture that listens to the story of God and seeks our place in that story rather than pulling out random verses as proof texts for our particular brand of faith, our distinctive sets of doctrines.

The truth is that looking back on past history and recognizing flaws in thinking and performance is not new and not particularly difficult. Hindsight is nearly always 20/20. We can see what was right about Martin Luther's break with the Roman Catholic Church. We can understand why the King James Version was such a cultural landmark for Western Civilization. We can discover the roots of Enlightenment thinking and democracy in American church history.

Of course, what all of us seem most able and inclined to do is to critique the church of our own experience. Whether it was legalism or exclusivism or racism or moral-ethical license, we know how to label the failures of others and ourselves. The institutional model had all of those flaws. But the truth is that there is no blessing in complaining bitterly about the past. It serves no good purpose to condemn our forbears for being people of their time and cultural circumstances. True, we do not ignore past sin with its generational repercussions. But we also do not excuse ourselves by blaming the past. The past is of value to us as our teacher, helping us to learn and become what we are called to be in the present.

The Meaning of "Relational Faith"

In our time and in our circumstances, we seek to hold up a version of Christianity that looks to Jesus and defines Christian unity in relationship to him. We offer a model that focuses our eyes on Jesus, that points other people to Jesus, that means an entire life of giving glory to God because of our lived experiences of Jesus. So what does that look like that's any different from what we're already doing?

In some cases, it looks no different at all. To the degree that anyone already finds her identity in Christ and his empowerment through the Holy Spirit and their sense of community and place on this planet in a relationship to Christ, this proposal is already at work. But let me suggest some ways in which this kind of focus on Jesus can have a life-changing impact on the day-to-day life of faith for many of us.

For one thing, it means that we rethink, recreate, and renew our identity as Christ-ians (i.e., Christ-followers, Christ-ones), as those who have been clothed with Christ. We take seriously the claims of Paul that all who are in Christ have died to sin

> *My parents were content with me if I tried to do as well as I could what I was able to do. I wasn't compared with others whether they were more gifted than I or less gifted. That seems like sound common sense, sound psychology and sound Christianity.*
>
> –Andrew M. Greeley

and have been raised to life by the power of the Holy Spirit. We share with Paul the conviction that we have been crucified with Christ and no longer live—but Christ lives in us. We also recognize that such an identity is not a matter of human performance or skillful human reasoning; it is the gift of the Living God who still is active in our world and in our lives. We find our identity and security not in the American economy and our growing collection of stuff, not in the pride of our own performance or the arrogance of our superior intellects, not in a particular name brand of church, but in the mind of Christ. We find our places in the continuing story of Jesus, understanding that we have been called to be Jesus—to be the living Christ in our world. We live in the Gospel accounts of Jesus and the lives of the early Christians, not to restore an ancient pattern but to understand our own calling to be Jesus today. As the earliest Christians were empowered to be Jesus in the first century, we are now empowered to be Jesus in the twenty-first century.

That renewed identity in Christ, empowered by the indwelling presence of the Holy Spirit, makes us the sacred space of God on this planet. It is Spirit presence that allows us to exchange the need to think right and be right for the love of authentic living. Again, the need to have all the right answers was and is a cultural reading tied to competition and winning. When "winning is everything" culturally, that same understanding rubs off on churches. So bigger is better: the church with the biggest facility wins, the church with the most right answers wins, the church that has the most daily Bible readers wins, and so on.

Identity in Christ, however, means losing one's life for his sake. It means that our Christian identity is as real on Monday or Thursday as it is on Sunday morning. It means that we don't become anonymous believers inside or outside of a particular church building. It means Christ lives in us in our family settings and in our workplaces and in our recreation. There is no place where we are not on our spiritual journey. It certainly doesn't mean we are perfect; this is not a journey in which we suddenly leave confusion and dysfunction behind and wake up the next morning to contentment and perfection. It is a journey in which we cycle through victories and defeats, in which we break down beside the road and have to have emergency assistance sometimes. But we no longer have to hide the reality of those moments. Our new cultural context demands authenticity, reality. For those of you who can remember the old television show *Quincy*, compare that coroner's office to *C.S.I.* Or compare the World War II movie *The Longest Day* to *Saving Private Ryan*. Authentic is "in"!

Focusing on Jesus and sharing in the mind of Christ means that particular manifestations of the body of Christ, particular groupings of kingdom people, are called to be safe places in the neighborhood. The local church is where we find safe people who listen and care and walk alongside to encourage one another. It's not where the intact people are isolated from the broken people; it's where those once broken now bind each other's wounds. It is where people tell the truth about their lives, knowing that only the pain of truth-telling can bring release and freedom.

Our proposal to focus on Jesus means that Scripture is no longer a set of proof-texts or a collection of facts or God's rulebook for human behavior. Scripture is the unfolding story of God acting both to create and to re-create. It is not an easy book to understand. It was never intended as a document to be individually read and interpreted—a sort of correspondence course in salvation. Prior to the invention of the printing press, access to the content of Scripture was oral. For thousands of years it could only be heard and interpreted in the context of community. Yes, individuals could comment on Scripture, but those comments were always for the larger hearing of the community. Only after there was individual access did there become an opportunity for an individual, isolated reading and interpretation that had no need or use for community.

Just as identity in Christ is always community identity, our reading of Scripture becomes a community reading as well. While we still have access to reading as individuals, we stop asking, "What does this mean to me?"—as though there is such an isolated meaning. Instead we have a group mentality that asks, "What does this mean to us?" More importantly, we lay aside individual interpretations precisely because they are inevitably argumentative and divisive. We give up the right of individual interpretation and take on the accountability of shared reading. This is not a pooling of collective ignorance. The Bible is full of stories from ancient and often quite alien cultural settings and belief systems, and we cannot ignore those differences. So we listen to the voices of scholarship just as we listen to the child who intuitively hears what God is saying in a particular story.

> *As we go to the cradle only in order to find the baby, so we go to the Scriptures only to find Christ.*
>
> –Martin Luther

One of the great ironies of our usual reading of Scripture can be seen in the ways we have used Romans 14. Clearly Paul writes these words to help diffuse tension between the "strong" and the "weak" in the community. It is clear that both sides (whoever they are) are called to humility and acceptance and are being asked to lay aside the judgmental attitudes that lead to mutual rejection rather than mutual edification. Too often today, this text is brought up in divisive contexts, to be sure, but the debate is only heightened by its use since both sides will choose the weaker brother or stronger brother side and use it for power and control—and thereby "winning." How often do we hear the claim of conscience and "weakness" used as a means of thwarting the objectionable actions of another? Neither side is interested in humility and submission; both sides desire the power and control that comes from preserving their current interpretation or practice. At the heart of this reading is still that need to define the rules of human behavior rather than a pursuit of being Jesus to one another. The result is not greater humility in community but yet another power play among disagreeable individuals.

A Christ-centered community reading of Scripture means we can hear the we-language of Romans 14 centering our community life: "We do not live to ourselves, and we do not die to ourselves. If we live, we live to the Lord, and if we die, we die to the Lord; so then, whether we live or whether we die, we are the Lord's" (Rom.14:7-8). It is our shared identity in Christ that empowers the move beyond judgmental attitudes to mutual edification (Rom.14:10-23).

Finally, a relational understanding of our faith transforms evangelism from winning a debate or argument with those "lost" souls into service and conversation with friends. You see, in the institutional model evangelism became a sales pitch, and conversion was like scoring the winning touchdown. We beat the other guys. We had the superior argument, the better proof-texts. We generated the more polished speech that demonstrated we were right and they were wrong. Please understand the caricature being employed here. I know I am overstating the case. Not all evangelism was done to win an argument. Not all evangelism employed fear and scare tactics and a debate mentality. But the need to be right meant others had to be wrong. Categories of superior and inferior were subconsciously built into the effort to save the lost. Even the word "lost" took on an inferior cast. When Jesus came to seek and save the lost, as he describes them in those parables of Luke 15, the lost are those who were valued and loved and missed by the group. A relational approach to God through Jesus means treating all people as Jesus treated people.

Yes, Jesus became argumentative at times. But with whom? Not the outsiders, not the ones already feeling outcast and distanced from God and the group. Jesus became argumentative with those who made exclusivist claims—those insiders who thought they were more righteous, more religious than other people.

I know that people have been talking and writing about friendship evangelism for years. Even then it often felt, to me at least, as if it was a new and better sales pitch. What I'm trying to describe here is a desire to have relationships with other people through which people encounter Jesus in us. We serve cups of cold water with no ulterior motive other than to offer them the love of Christ. There is no "bait-and-switch" plan for getting them indoctrinated. We come alongside to serve and befriend and allow Jesus to be seen through us. As people find us to be safe people, people of integrity they can trust, they begin to share the journey.

Conclusion

It's hard in the world of our time and place to find something other than tabloid relationships. People are sometimes interested in us only for the sake of gossip or innuendo or some personal exploitation that makes them feel better about themselves. But what of someone who listens, who doesn't try to fix my life with easy answers? What of one who comes alongside my life and hears me? Rather than offering answers, he asks clarifying questions. And he stays as I work through them in my own muddleheaded way. That's what Jesus did. He rarely responded with answers; he loved reframing the circumstances with questions.

Perhaps this illustration will help, especially since one of the things that draws believers together regularly is worship and praise in song. I love music. I love to sing. When I was a child in church, I never wanted to grow up and be a preacher like my Dad. I wanted to be the song leader! I love being in worship assemblies on Sundays for the music. I have long believed that our notions of God and worship are shaped more by the music than by the preaching.

I attended a conference recently in which the conversation was about preaching, but one person made a striking observation about how people experience God in our time. He reflected on the history of the church. For a millennium—roughly between 500 and 1500—the church experienced God through liturgy, through the Catholic Mass. With the Protestant reformation, the emphasis among Protestants at least shifted to experiencing God through the Word—through Scripture and through preaching. But in the past quarter of a century, as we experience the Postmodern shift, people now experience God—young people, especially—through musical liturgy again.

I go through most of my days with some kind of song rattling around in my brain. Most of the time, I find myself thinking the words or the music of songs that I really like. Sometimes they are Christian songs, sometimes songs from the radio or a movie that I recently watched. Most of us, even if we are tone deaf, have those moments in our lives where the words and music of a particular song get stuck in our brains. So we find ourselves doing a variety of things with that song playing inside. There are those songs that come to mind that we don't even like sometimes, and we still can't get rid of them.

> *It is time that Christians were judged more by their likeness to Christ than their notions of Christ.*
>
> –Lucretia Mott

There are other songs that overwhelm us the first time we hear them, and we never get tired of them.

Think of the Jesus Proposal as God's new song for our lives. Only it's not just one tune—that's the marvel of music. You would think that with a limited number of notes on the scale, sooner or later songwriters would run out of tunes. But they don't! Yes, there are repeated rhythms and note progressions; sometimes the same tune is used with different words. But music has the capacity to be fresh, to be renewed—even in its sameness. Music can take on such radically different styles, and few of us appreciate or understand every style. But something powerful is communicated to different people through the vast variety of forms.

I know the analogy is not perfect. But think of the Jesus Proposal as this single lyric being given the appropriate music for every heart. When you first begin to hear all of the different sounds, it is rather chaotic. You can't make sense of the music line. But the more you listen, the more the chaos turns into God's glorious symphony—with every note having its place, every song part of a larger whole, but always with a common lyric.

We are abundantly blessed to live in a time of new songs—of a new song that God wants to place in our heads and on our hearts. A song that shouts to the Lord! A song whose lyrics bring good news and whose music line instills life in every heart. Don't you think we should try to sing along?

Notes

1. Brian McLaren, *More Ready Than You Realize: Evangelism as Dance in the Postmodern Matrix* (Grand Rapids: Zondervan, 2002), p. 34; cf. Jaroslav Pelikan, *Jesus Through the Centuries* (New York: Harper & Row, 1985) in which a respected historian and theologian documents the array of culturally-shaped portraits of Jesus across the centuries that often tell more about the temper and values of the age that produced them than about the Nazarene.

2. See Mark Noll's compelling discussion of the influence of American republicanism and what he calls a "reformed literal hermeneutic" of

Protestantism in America in the early nineteenth century. Much of our particular understanding of Scripture as a "blueprint" and our judicial reading of texts can be traced to the larger unfolding of political and religious history in the early days of American democracy. See *America's God* (New York: Oxford University, 2002), pp. 367-385.

Just think, every promise God has ever made finds its fulfillment in Jesus. God doesn't just give us grace, He gives us Jesus, the Lord of grace. If it's peace, it's only found in Jesus, the Prince of Peace. Even life itself is found in the Resurrection and the Life. Christianity isn't all that complicated. . . it's Jesus.

–Joni Eareckson Tada

7. BEING GOD'S CHILD: EVENT OR PROCESS?

Rubel Shelly

Much of the division among Christians is over key *events* of Christian experience. For example, some churches practice what is called "closed communion." They restrict participation in the Lord's Supper to those who hold membership in their own denomination or those who have already received baptism or those who subscribe to certain articles of faith. At certain times and places in Christian history, one had to submit to an examination of his or her faith by a person or panel of church officials prior to a time of communion. Those judged worthy to participate were then given a token that would admit them to the communion table.

Baptism has also caused a great deal of division. Because of certain New Testament texts about the relationship of baptism to Christ or spiritual rebirth or remission of sins, baptism has normally been associated with membership in the Christian community and/or salvation. Depending on the mode (i.e., sprinkling, pouring, immersion) or one's age (i.e., infant, young child, adult) at baptism, a given group might not honor a person's baptism. She might be excluded from membership in a given church. Or she might be judged unsaved.

This approach—identifying a single event or ceremony as the badge of Christian identity and spiritual kinship—is fully consistent with Modernity. It provides a formula for including some and excluding others. It draws a clear line between those deemed worthy of acceptance and those to be left out of the community. I'm not at all sure this is how things worked in the earliest days of the church.

> *In the spiritual journey we travel through the night toward the day. We walk not in the bright sunshine of total certainty but through the darkness of ignorance, error, muddle and uncertainty. We make progress in the journey as we grow in faith.*
>
> – Christopher Bryant

In a Postmodern world, lines of demarcation are a bit more blurred than they were in the period of Modernity. In the more extreme forms of Postmodern thought, that blurriness is a bad thing. No action is really good or bad; everything is relative to a culture or circumstance. There is no ultimate distinction between truth and error; you have your truth, and I have mine. In such varieties of Postmodern relativism, Christianity is neither better nor worse than Islam or Buddhism, agnosticism or atheism. One should remember, however, that moral and epistemological relativism was embraced by Modernity as well.

The healthier side of Postmodernity's rejection of rigid formulas in favor of blurred lines of distinction is not difficult to see and appreciate. Blacks and whites, rich and poor, scholars and illiterates, citizens and refugees—all can have a seat at the same table of opportunity. There will be less class consciousness. There will be fewer acts of unjust discrimination and intolerance.

Within the context of Christian discussion, I am encouraged rather than frightened by what I have called the "healthier side of Postmodernity's rejection of rigid formulas." It could very well move believers in Christ away from institutional models of church to an organic model. Christians might think less about institutional religion and more about the body of Christ, less about denominational distinctions and more about organic ties to one another. If that should happen, we might learn to think, speak, and live more as the church did in its early history than it has of late. If it should happen, we just might be more like Christ's original vision for his church.

In particular, what if—in good biblical and Postmodern fashion—we thought of salvation more as a process than an event? What if we understood spiritual transformation as something that takes place over time rather than instantly? What if we used biblical figures of speech like "pilgrimage" and "birth" rather than "church member" and "getting saved"? In other words, what if we were retrained so that we no longer looked to a single event like the sinner's prayer, immersion, or a church vote to validate someone's status as a Christian but to the direction and tone of his life over time? What if we looked for direction rather than perfection in one another's spiritual life?

After all, I've known people who have been baptized but who use God's name in profane ways or abuse their children or mouth and model racism. Is the event of their baptism enough to offset their way of life? Is church membership sufficient to compensate for moral and spiritual failure? On the other hand, I know people whose baptism is defective on my understanding of the Bible but whose passion for God and uprightness of character left no doubt that they were light-years more Christ-like than I am. Should I judge them to be lost? May I reasonably doubt that God's grace could cover some defect in their theology yet trust it to absolve my pride or selfishness?

The Deficiency of Event-Based Religion

This generation is not the first to observe that event-based religion can be shallow and unconvincing. Did reformers such as Luther not protest the idea that prayers and ritual could be substituted for holiness? No less than Alexander Campbell wrestled with this same issue in the "second reformation" of which he was a leading figure. This was his comment on the matter:

> Should I find a Pedobaptist more intelligent in the Christian Scriptures, more spiritually-minded and more devoted to the Lord than a Baptist, or one immersed on a profession of the ancient faith, I could not hesitate a moment in giving the preference of my heart to him that loveth most. Did I act otherwise, I would be a pure sectarian, a Pharisee among Christians. Still I will be asked, How do I know that any one loves my Master but by his obedience to his

commandments? I answer, In no other way. But mark, I do not substitute obedience to one commandment, for universal or even for general obedience. And should I see a sectarian Baptist or a Pedobaptist more spiritually-minded, more generally conformed to the requisitions of the Messiah, than one who precisely acquiesces with me in the theory or practice of immersion as I teach, doubtless the former rather than the latter, would have my cordial approbation and love as a Christian. So I judge, and so I feel. It is the image of Christ the Christian looks for and loves; and this does not consist in being exact in a few items, but in general devotion to the whole truth as far as known.

With me mistakes of the understanding and errors of the affections are not to be confounded. They are as distant as the poles. An angel may mistake the meaning of a commandment, but he will obey it in the sense in which he understands it. John Bunyan and John Newton were very different persons, and had very different views of baptism, and of some other things; yet they were both disposed to obey, and to the extent of their knowledge did obey the Lord in every thing.

There are mistakes with, and without depravity. There are wilful errors which all the world must condemn, and unavoidable mistakes which every one will pity. The Apostles mistook the Saviour when he said concerning John, "What if I will that John tarry till I come;" but the Jews perverted his words when they alleged that Abraham had died, in proof that he

spake falsely when he said, "If a man keep my word
he shall never see death."

Many a good man has been mistaken. Mistakes
are to be regarded as culpable and as declarative of
a corrupt heart only when they proceed from a wilful neglect of the means of knowing what is commanded. Ignorance is always a crime when it is vol-
untary; and innocent when it is involuntary. Now,
unless I could prove that all who neglect the positive
institutions of Christ and have substituted for them
something else of human authority, do it knowingly,
or, if not knowingly, are voluntarily ignorant of what
is written, I could not, I dare not say that their mistakes are such as unchristianize all their professions.[1]

More than a century and a half later—and long after many of
us had fixed on an event we considered definitive of conversion—we have come full circle to the question yet again
in the larger Christian culture. Writing to his fellow youth
ministers, one has tried to explain the shift in mindset on
evangelism between Modernity and Postmodernity.

For the last few centuries, evangelism was considered mainly a cognitive process (i.e., Christianity is
a set of propositions an individual must intellectually
agree with and accept as true.) But more recently, the
understanding of conversion has been shifting
toward the transformation of the whole person. In
fact, in the postmodern context, it could be said that
we ought to first evangelize experientially and teach
the content of the faith later! After all, Jesus says to

his disciples, "Follow me!"—not "Do you accept me as your personal Lord and Savior?"[2]

Jones' term for what I have dubbed "event-based religion" is reductionism. He writes of the tendency to purchase a program, use a particular educational curriculum, or—in what should be easily recognized among Churches of Christ—to "take our kids to a really hyped-up rally rather than do the long, hard work of building relationships and sharing Christ over time."[3]

The comment about emotional youth rallies reminds me of one of the meanest human beings I have ever known who was worried that his son was seventeen, about to graduate from high school, and leave home. His last hope, as he saw it, was the final summer revival meeting his little church would be sponsoring before his boy was gone. He wanted the elders of that church to be sure the meetings were "strong"—so his son would be baptized. He was convinced that his boy needed to be baptized. He had never seen the young man's great need to live within a family where he and his mother were not terrorized by him. He was hoping against reason that he could replace the process of training that can lead a child to Christ with an

> *Every man has two journeys to make through life. There is the outer journey, with its various incidents and the milestones. There is also an inner journey, a spiritual Odyssey, with a secret history of its own.*
>
> – William Ralph Inge

event that would save him—and give his father peace of mind that he had "done all he could" or "everything neces- sary" for the boy.

Out of my own life experience, I have wrestled with this event-versus-process view of salvation and discipleship. I was baptized when I was twelve years old, but I had no clear understanding of either baptism or Jesus Christ at the time. My view of baptism was legalistic and transactional to the core. That is, I had been taught by evangelists who came through our little town that the cross was "God's part" to sal- vation and that baptism was "our part." The transaction of God's offer was complete only when we "added our part" to the equation. With horror at such an understanding now, I visualize a vending machine and hear the *ka-ching* of the transaction as I write about it! I lived long enough to learn the gospel and understand that baptismal regeneration is a false doctrine. In the same process—there's that word again —of growth and clarification, I also learned that the "gift of the Holy Spirit" in Acts 2:38 was not the Bible but the Holy Spirit in his personal presence.

How much more confused and wrong-headed could a baptismal theology be? How much farther from the truth of Scripture could I have been when I was immersed in that cold water on a hot July night? When I get to heaven, maybe I'll want to ask God when I was really saved. Was it when I got clear on the Holy Spirit at about twenty-one or -two? Was it when I finally grasped the grace-nature of the gospel in my thirties? I suspect he will tell me there was no "moment at which" I was saved—but that he sought and found me through the entire process.

The New Testament employs several metaphors of salvation and entrance into the family of God. No one of them is exhaustive. Each of them adds insight to the total picture of a process that is God's own rather than ours. One or two of the more familiar metaphors of Scripture may help clarify how one can grasp salvation as an inclusive process rather than any single event. Better still, a look at these biblical figures will help one appreciate this divine work as a process with distinct events that will be expected along the way.

Analogy: Conception, Birth, and Growth

Is there anyone who is not in awe of the continuous miracle of physical birth? Distinct events mark the developmental process that produces a live birth. Wonderful and beautiful process that it is, it is not free of ambiguity. With regard to the ethical position one stakes out on abortion, for example, these ambiguities are quite significant. They generate heated debates on the exact time at which the life in process from conception to viability to birth to early development in a family should be thought of as a child (i.e., fully human).

By a process of sexual union, an egg is *fertilized*. At the instant of conception, the mother and father contribute one-half complement each of the genetic material that will define forever many of the attributes of their child. The newly formed cell with its own unique genetic content is now called a *zygote* and begins a long process of development. The first cell division takes approximately thirty hours. Then, with increasing speed, cell replication continues until—after four or five days—a hollow, fluid-filled ball called a *blastocyst* is formed. The cells on the outside provide a protective covering from this point forward, while the ones on the inside (i.e., the embryonic disk) produce the new person.

For a period ranging from about the second week through the eighth, the term of reference becomes *embryo*. In this period of incredibly rapid and complex development, human form becomes visible. A tiny heart begins pumping, internal organs form, and tiny arms and legs—even fingers and toes—become distinguishable. By the end of two months from conception, the tiny baby is moving about and responding to the womb's environment. Yet the mother cannot even feel a presence inside her own body because the organism is still so tiny.

By the time mom and dad get their first ultrasound photo to show around among family and friends at maybe three months, their baby—in spite of all the incredible things that have happened in his or her development—is still only about one inch long and weighs only about one ounce. They may or may not find out from their ultrasound whether to paint the nursery pink or blue!

By the fourth month, she is big enough and moving around enough to let her mother know she is there! Mom feels her moving in her womb. Those first movements a mother senses are called *quickening*. Dad will soon enough be able to feel his daughter kick and move now. And within another thirty days, she is even responding to light as well as other external stimuli.

Millions of people around the world have seen the photograph of 21-week-old Samuel Armas that was taken at Vanderbilt University Medical Center in Nashville in the fall of 1999. Dr. Joseph Bruner operated on him in hopes of alleviating the effects of spina bifida. This staged photo shows Samuel's tiny hand grasping the surgeon's finger by reflex action. The surgery was successful, and Samuel was born in December of that year. He is developing well—much to the delight of his parents.

Sometime between twenty-two and twenty-six weeks, these tiny, frail-looking babies reach *viability*—the point at which they can first survive outside their mother's wombs. But the ideal situation is, of course, for the baby to develop for a full nine months in that God-designed protective environment. Then she can make her dynamic presence known to beaming-but-soon-to-be-sleepless parents and doting-and-ready-to-spoil-her-rotten grandparents.

So tell me: *At what point was this living being a human being?* There is hardly universal agreement on how to answer that question. A few would say the life was human only after birth. There are even some who, with Peter Singer and Aristotle, would claim that a child outside the womb is not human and does not have rights until at least several months after birth. More would likely say viability. Then there are those of us who insist that—even though we cannot say with certainty that the conceptus is truly and fully "human" at that point—fetal life should be valued and protected from the point of conception forward. Ours is called a very conservative point of view on the value of human life. So be it.

Application: Conception, Birth, and Growth

The point of this exercise in human fetal development is more about our presenting issue of spiritual birth and identity than the abortion controversy. At what point in one's journey to spiritual life do we count him or her a Christian—the word simply means "Christ-follower" or "one who gives allegiance to Christ"—and extend our fellowship as the body of

Christ? Is it at repentance and saying the sinner's prayer? Is it in the event of his or her hearing the gospel with a receptive heart, the Good News that Jesus saved? Is it at the point of one's initial, private acknowledgment of faith? Or perhaps the initial confession of that faith? Is water baptism in the name of Jesus the defining moment of union with Christ?

> *The Church is not a finished, solidly built and furnished house, in which all that changes is the successive generations who live in it. The Church is a living reality which has had a history of its own and still has one.*
>
> –Karl Rahner

Is one saved only at the point of the manifest presence of the Holy Spirit in his life? Or is one a Christian only after he has begun sharing in the life of the church? Should there be a time of nurture by the Word of God and prayer that must be accounted for before one can be regarded as a child of God? Or must she be able to prove the genuineness of her faith through the discipline of life in Christ—including the willingness to suffer for her faith? I suspect the right answer may be "Yes"—to all of these questions rather than to any one.

I know this much for sure: Contrary to the abortion issue in which it is considered ethically "conservative" to honor and protect a developing child from the beginning, it is often considered theologically "liberal" in my heritage to take the same attitude toward emerging spiritual life. Thus I have listened to grown men debate this question: If a contrite believer in Christ is killed in an automobile wreck on the way to the river for baptism, can he be saved? Is water baptism definitive for God's redemptive work? Or is it a sign of spiritual cleansing in a larger process? Whether reflecting on the creative miracle of God in producing physical or spiritual life, I prefer to affirm, nurture, and protect that life from its earliest formation. From the first evidence of passion for Jesus all the way to the maturity of a Christian who is willing to die for the holy name he wears, God is at work in the total process. And I want to be careful not to impede (i.e., abort) what God is at work to accomplish.

Our fondness born of Modernity to have a single formula that fits every situation doesn't work well either with the New Testament data or with spiritual pilgrims in the real world. I think that is so because salvation is not an event but a journey, not a single "moment at which" but a *pilgrim direction* toward God.

The notion of salvation as rebirth into the family of God certainly supports this view. How can we preach, for example, the importance—even necessity—of the baptismal event for salvation and regard others who have not been immersed as brothers and sisters in the family of God? How can we say we affirm the theological importance of baptism and extend spiritual fellowship to those who are still unbaptized? We would argue that it is wrong to deny fellowship to anyone who gives evidence of seeking God in good faith through Jesus Christ—and thereby become a stumbling block to his continued growth and development in spiritual life. Making baptism, church membership, or repentance of a particular action into *the* test of Christian fellowship is inconsistent with

Christ's example of receiving those whom the institutional faith of his own time had deemed unworthy and runs contrary to the biblical evidence.

Is spiritual rebirth from above not described in the New Testament in process terms? Consider the following texts before committing yourself to a single "moment at which" one can be considered a Christian (i.e., Christ-follower) and participate in the fellowship of the family of God. "If you know that he is righteous, you may be sure that everyone who does right has been born of him" (1 John 2:29). "Beloved, let us love one another, because love is from God; everyone who loves is born of God and knows God" (1 John 4:7). "Everyone who believes that Jesus is the Christ has been born of God, and everyone who loves the parent loves the child" (1 John 5:1). "We know that those who are born of God do not sin, but the one who was born of God protects them, and the evil one does not touch them" (1 John 5:18).

These few texts all come from the epistle of 1 John. Suppose now that we add the Gospel of John. We find Jesus saying this to Nicodemus: "Very truly, I tell you, no one can enter the kingdom of God without being born of water and Spirit" (John 3:5). Adding the writings of Peter to those of John, we find this text on the same subject of spiritual rebirth: "You have been born anew, not of perishable but of imperishable seed, through the living and enduring word of God" (1 Pet.1:23).

Are we just trying to confuse you with these verses? Are we trying to set up a situation where each denomination can choose its favorite verses and build a doctrine of the new birth around the texts of its choice? Not at all! We are trying instead to protest and prevent that sort of thing. We are warning against the further perpetuation of *faith* as the Baptist doctrine, *baptism* as the Church of Christ doctrine, and the *Holy Spirit* as Pentecostal doctrine. Baptists have stressed faith in order to say that salvation is God's work alone—never our achievement through obedience or any combination of good works—and can be received only by trusting his grace; they have not resisted baptism—it's in their name!—but what they perceived us to say that turned baptism into a human good work we bartered for salvation. Pentecostals have generally affirmed the necessity of water baptism but have insisted that the regenerating power of God is not water but Spirit; they have pleaded the case for Spirit-presence as the ultimate sign of God's saving work in a believer's life.

So how is someone "born of God" today? When does someone become a child of God? When should we regard a person as a member of God's spiritual family?

Repentance is often the initial event in which one begins to seek God. She sees that her life is miserable and wretched in sin and cries out for God. She turns her heart away from the world and begins to seek him. That is the precise moment at which God wants one of us who knows the story to tell her the Good News about Jesus. In a teaching event, she learns that God's love became flesh in pursuit of her in Jesus of Nazareth and that his death on Calvary was in her place. Christ Jesus was made sin for her so that she might become righteous in him. In hearing that message, her heart is captured by God's love. She now has faith that Christ alone can save her.

She is intelligent enough to ask her teacher, "So what should I do now that I believe in Jesus?" Whether Baptist, Church of Christ, or Pentecostal, nobody is going to tell her the process has ended at faith. It has only begun! Now she needs to hear the Pauline baptismal language about dying and rising with Christ. She will be told about the presence and power of the Holy Spirit to set her free from her old way of life. Somebody will need to stress the importance of a community of fellow believers in which she can grow to maturity. That is where she will be nurtured in the Word of God, prayer, and Christian fellowship. And somebody will need to help her understand that even suffering for her newfound faith is a discipline to character and the chance to participate with Christ in his suffering for us.

> *The best measure of a spiritual life is not its ecstasies but its obedience.*
>
> –Oswald Chambers

If we follow the analogy of physical birth for this process of spiritual birth, which makes more sense: To protect and nurture as new life from the earliest moment or only from the later ones? To wait for fuller development before regarding her as a Christian? Or to claim, nurture, and protect from the very earliest point of faith in and love for Christ? "The Lord knows those who are his" (2 Tim.2:19b), and I am willing to leave all judgment to him. So, while granting God alone the right to answer the question about those who are his own, I prefer to run the risk of extending my acceptance, encouragement, and love to those who may be only "near" the kingdom of God than to exclude even one whom he has accepted.

Law vs. Grace

The penchant for event-based theories of salvation is not only characteristic of Modernity over against Postmodernity but of a law-based theory of salvation.

Within a law-based system, salvation is predicated upon keeping commandments. And, to be sure, baptism—like repentance, faith, prayer, willingness to suffer for Christ, and many other things associated with salvation—is a commandment of God. But the great frustration of all those of us who have ever sought new life and assurance through legalism is that our obedience is always incomplete and flawed. There can be no redemption on the basis of law, "for whoever keeps the whole law but fails in one point has become accountable for all of it" (Jas. 2:10). Out of his own past and his search for God through law, Paul declared the impossibility of justification through rule-keeping (Rom. 3:20). What was impossible for him is not the goal for us. Surely his experience was included in the biblical record for the sake of warning us against making the same mistake.

Under a grace-based approach, those of us whose obedience to commandments is flawed can still rejoice in the security of salvation in Christ Jesus. After the example of Abraham, we are accounted righteous through faith rather than through performance, on the basis of God's goodness rather than our own. Righteousness was credited to Abraham because of his faith and in spite of a flawed obedience. Furthermore, Paul stresses that it was not after his circumcision but before it that he was declared righteous before the Lord (Rom. 4:9-12).

Surely the reason why Christianity has so often been perverted into a law-based religion is that some of the most godly of people fear that the motivation for obedience will be eroded if grace is emphasized over law. While granting that a perverse heart may be looking for any excuse to evade the reign of God in his heart and life, legalism will not rescue that heart.

To the contrary, it plays into its hands by distinguishing "essential" and "non-essential" elements of the faith. It leads people to think they can be saved by being right on their doctrine of church organization and worship—while barring African-Americans from their church because of their racism! It causes them to think that correctness on baptism or the Lord's Supper somehow compensates for being greedy or abusive or sexist!

Faith, on the other hand, will not excuse itself from the authority of God. Faith and works go together as root and fruit, not as failure and fullness or start and finish (Jas. 2:18ff). Saving faith always welcomes new information, new insight, and new events of surrender. It has no need to be defensive in its need to grow, express itself, and obey.

Conclusion

For some, salvation is an event marked by what is commonly called "the sinner's prayer." For others, the critical moment at which one is saved is marked by the waters of baptism. For still others, the defining occurrence is a life-transforming experience of the Holy Spirit. *Which is it?* Have you ever seen a multiple-choice question on an exam with the option: "all of the above"? Or what about this very Postmodern option: "none of the above—but a relationship that grows over time"?

What if one never completes this process? Dies after the second or fourth or sixth step? We can trust God to do right by such a man or woman, don't you think? He knows our hearts and will judge by a fullness of knowledge you and I can't have.

In the interval between our stumbling attempts at seeking God and the final Judgment, I can live with my brothers and sisters who put one event above another in their experience. I understand from my own experience that there are key moments and events that have been defining to me but which have played a far less significant role in someone else's spiritual life. It is not, after all, any single event but the total process of following Jesus that is our experience of God's grace.

On the authority of the apostle Paul, we may say that Christians are those who "have been saved," "are being saved," and "will be saved" at his return (cf. Eph.2:8; 1 Cor.1:18; Rom.5:9-10). This glorious process and all the event-markers along the way are God's work in us—past, present, and future; complete and ongoing. What a wonder of grace that God would invest himself so completely in our needs and bring us to glory in his Son through the power of the Holy Spirit.

Notes

1. Alexander Campbell, "Any Christians Among Protestant Parties, *Millennial Harbinger* (September 1837): 412; available online at http://www.bible.acu.edu/stone-campbell/Etexts/lun16.html.

2. Tony Jones, *Postmodern Youth Ministry: Exploring Cultural Shift, Cultivating Authentic Community, Creating Holistic Connections* (Grand Rapids: Zondervan, 2001), p.111. "We are working with students who are bombarded with the message of Jesus at rallies, on TV, by us and their parents, and at church on Sunday morning—and it's almost exclusively with words. Instead, let's invite kids into the Body of Christ, into a community that lives out the moral imperatives of Scripture. In that way, we'll be evangelizing postmodern kids in a postmodern way. Just as the Word became

flesh and dwelt among us, our youth groups—as Christ's Body—must 'flesh out' the gospel message. Many of us have told students that it doesn't matter if you go to church or not to be saved, it only matters if you've accepted Jesus into your heart. In fact, salvation is a lot more complex than that—it's more of a process, more mysterious and less definable than we might think." Ibid., p.118.

3. Ibid., p. 124.

The Christian faith is the most exciting drama that ever staggered the imagination. . . . That drama is summarized quite clearly in the creeds of the Church, and if we think it dull it is because we either have never really read those amazing documents or have recited them so often and so mechanically as to have lost all sense of their meaning. The plot pivots upon a single character, and the whole action is the answer to a single central problem: What think ye of Christ?

–Dorothy L. Sayers

8. THE PROPOSAL AT WORK

Rubel Shelly

More and more people in the United States seem to have decided they can live without church.[1] But be careful that you don't misinterpret the meaning of that fact. It means something different in a Postmodern world than it would have meant to someone rooted in Modernity.

True enough, there are larger-than-ever numbers of Americans who say they are agnostic or atheist with regard to the existence of God. But those numbers still remain relatively low. Depending on the poll you cite, somewhere between 90% and 96% of people in this country still say they believe in a personal deity. Yet church attendance generally and identification with particular denominations hardly reflect so high a percentage of citizens. Only about 30% to 32% attend religious services on a weekly basis. Significantly higher percentages say they read the Bible or pray regularly. People are telling us they believe in God, read their Bibles, and pray; but those same people who say *they cannot live without God* are nonetheless telling us *they can live without church.* If such a thought was outlandish to Moderns, it is not at all intimidating to Postmoderns.

So what are we to make of these facts? Are they simply a jumble of inconsistent statistics? Perhaps the category "spiritual but not religious" that was used in a January 2002 *USA Today*/Gallup Poll helps a bit. It was a group experiencing significant growth in the survey. Spirituality is growing in America, but church attendance and membership generally are not. In a region of the country where religion—defined as an organized denomination or faith-group—has the lowest percentage of involvement, one 31-year-old churchgoer offered an explanation of the behavior of his peers. "I totally understand my friends who hate church or think it's boring or react negatively because of the formalities and customs," he said. "They think it's strange, stuffy, weird and ritualistic."[2]

People who are searching for God don't believe they are being helped in their quest by the church. The church has become an obstacle to them rather than a guide to God or a meaningful herald of the kingdom of God. Citizens of the world steeped in Modernity criticized the church, sometimes switched churches, but most often accepted the conclusion that God could not be found apart from the church; "spiritual but not religious" would have smacked of self-contradiction. Not so for Postmodern men and women; "spiritual but not religious" makes perfectly good sense to them—and is even a desirable option for increasing numbers of them. The problem is serious enough in today's new thought categories that the following question has been raised by the press: "Will religion survive the spirituality boom?"[3]

For people who take the Word of God seriously, these facts raise disturbing problems. We know that faith is meant to function within community. Lone Ranger faith is ultimately a fantasy—as well as an incongruity with Postmodernism's affirmation of community. God created us not only with social capabilities but nurtures and purifies faith within the community called church. Both the aggravations and joys of living a church experience contribute to the spiritual growth of every member of that fraternity. It's just like a nuclear family. As isolated individuals, we miss something that is required for personal growth.

So, even though many people have decided they can do without the church, God has chosen to make it an integral part of his will. But his original idea for how church would function was quite different from what has evolved over the centuries. What was intended to be a catalyst for spiritual life has become a hindrance to it in far too many instances. What we have dubbed "the Jesus proposal" is an attempt at clarifying how that original vision can be implemented in today's environment. In this chapter, we seek to trace out some of the particulars of the proposal.

Can the divided church we know only too well unite in any meaningful sense? Can believers in Christ surmount the petty divisiveness and sectarian rivalry that turn so many away from the church? Can it be a true community of faith? We believe it can but hasten to add that this has little or nothing to do with organizational union. We believe that denominational and non-denominational bodies of those who confess Jesus as their Lord can learn to honor a theological, relational, and missional unity that would both please God and make the church more attractive to those who have rejected it.

We believe it is possible for Christians of various traditions to link arms with one another without abandoning their identities or compromising the interpretations and practices that make them distinctive within the larger community of Christ-confessors. It is hard to conceive of something so foreign to our experience, but try to imagine what the Jesus proposal would look like in practice.

Theological Issues

Every Christian church embraces one or more doctrinal beliefs beyond faith in Jesus as Lord that makes it distinctive from other associations of believers. Should people in these various groups not be allowed the freedom to follow Scripture according to their good-faith attempts at interpretation and according to the liberty of their own consciences? Yet the history of the church shows that we have generally made each distinctive understanding into a new ground for division from brothers and sisters in Christ. Can we be distinctive without being divisive?

As a point of departure for addressing this issue, suppose we suggest that the Church of Christ is *a Bible-believing fellowship which affirms Jesus as the Son of God who died and was raised to atone for human sin and who gives eternal life to all those who are in him.* But that definition would not be enough for some people who use the term "Church of Christ" out of our background.

In more true-to-experience terms for us, it should be said that the Church of Christ is *a Bible-believing fellowship which affirms Jesus as the Son of God who died and was raised to atone for human sin and who gives eternal life to all those who are in him, rejects the five cardinal tenets of Calvinism, practices adult immersion for the remission of sins, participates in the Lord's Supper on a weekly basis, worships with a cappella music exclusively, organizes its local congregations under the oversight of a plurality of male elders, and embraces amillennial eschatology.*

To this already complex and cumbersome identification, others who come from a background like our own would insist on adding the following: *...pleads for the unity of the body of Christ among all who see each of the items already listed as it sees them, and believes that anyone who is not a member of one of its faithful-by-this-definition local congregations is in jeopardy of being lost.*

Theological light years separate these three attempts at characterizing the Church of Christ. The first is entirely biblical and fully sufficient to separate an entity from non-Christian groups. Yet it would be unsatisfactory for many people who are members of the Churches of Christ associated with what is known as the American Restoration Movement or the Stone-Campbell Movement. It is not "distinctive" enough for them. While it would serve quite well to distinguish its adherents from atheists, Buddhists, Muslims, and Mormons, it would not mark them off from the Baptist Church, Presbyterian Church, Pentecostal Church, and community churches. For those who make such an objection, two replies seem appropriate: (1) So what? (2) Does this description entail a loss of identity or require relinquishing any of our distinctive beliefs and practices?

First, think about the "So what?" response. It isn't intended to be flippant or funny. It is, instead, meant to be taken quite seriously. But it certainly isn't meant to be insulting either. Strictly from a biblical perspective, any group satisfying the standards of that first simple definition is a church that belongs to Christ—no matter what name is over its door or how garbled its doctrinal and/or moral life may be. Luke acknowledged a dozen people to be "disciples"[4] at Ephesus, even though their baptism was flawed (Acts 19:1-2). The church at Colossae had serious doctrinal heresy, and the church at Corinth was tolerating open immorality; both were nevertheless regarded as churches by a Spirit-guided Paul. No less than Jesus himself addressed a church that was "on the point of death" at Sardis only to affirm the "few persons" who had maintained the integrity of their faith in that setting (Rev. 3:1-6). By contrast, however, not even the original Jerusalem church or the great missionary church at Antioch would satisfy the second or third descriptions above.

> *Our doctrines are not photographs of Reality. They are the attempted description of heavenly things by means of the hints and guesses which earthly things provide.*
>
> –H. A. Williams

It should be apparent that anyone who feels compelled to replace the first definition for the church offered above for the sake of either alternative that follows is not defining the *New Testament Church of Christ* but the *Yellow Pages Church of Christ*. He has forsaken a very simple but *biblical identification* of the Church of Christ for a thoroughly *sectarian identification* of the Church of Christ. There is nothing peculiar to people from our heritage for doing so, for the same thing can be found not only in Roman Catholic literature but that of Baptists, Pentecostals, Presbyterians, and others.

Second, adopting the first simple characterization given above would in no way compromise or require the abandonment of the list of "distinctive" traits tacked to it in the second. It would only require instead that we distinguish between New Testament features and tradition-distinctive features of Churches of Christ in a particular time or cultural setting.[5] This is precisely what the early leaders in our movement envisioned in their language about "essentials" and "non-essentials" to the Christian faith. But we are so far removed from that ideal and so trapped within our received religious culture that we have not only lost that vision but no longer even speak of it in meaningful terms.

One may be committed to every single item in the second description (but not the third) and still avoid sectarian judgments. She may believe and teach them. He may argue for them. They may accept every implication of these positions for the life of a local church. But they are the distinctive requirements of a particular Christian heritage and not requirements for being a Christian, being a member of the body of Christ, and having the confident hope of heaven. The *divisiveness* that results from a sectarian penchant for judging and excluding others need not be the same as a commitment to the *distinctiveness* that arises inevitably from the interpretation of challenging texts in the New Testament literature.

At the beginning of this section, we stated that "every Christian church embraces one or more doctrinal beliefs beyond faith in Jesus as Lord that makes it distinctive from other associations of believers." And therein lies the root of the problem of sectarian division. What if we could manage to shift our thinking away from those "additional doctrinal beliefs" and focus on Jesus alone? What if we accepted a relational definition for the church instead of an institutional one? Is any issue beyond Christ himself important enough that it should be allowed to sever the fellowship of those who confess him as Lord?

What biblical text points us directly to a *theological anchor point* for believers concerned with preserving the unity of the church? Surely it is the core message of the gospel, what Paul said was "of first importance" to those he had led to Christ: "Now I would remind you, brothers and sisters, of the good news that I proclaimed to you, which you in turn received, in which also you stand, through which also you are being saved, if you hold firmly to the message that I proclaimed to you—unless you have come to believe in vain. For I handed on to you as of first importance what I in turn had received: that Christ died for our sins in accordance with the scriptures, and that he was buried, and that he was raised on the third day in accordance with the scriptures..." (1 Cor. 15:1-4).

Relational Issues

Imagine two die-hard supporters of any two football teams with an historic rivalry. Maybe one is a graduate of UCLA and the other of USC, Michigan and Notre Dame, or Texas A&M and the University of Texas. They sit on opposite sides of the field during a game. They cheer their respective schools. Each cherishes the camaraderie found in the section of the stadium reserved for people eager to declare their school loyalties. Yet they may be dear friends who ride to and from the game together and stop on the way home to have dinner. What a pity that interpretations about the millennium, worship, and church polity can separate disciples of Christ from one another so as to create mutually exclusive parties of sectarians!

Perhaps this illustration points to the fundamental problem of denominational rivalry leading to sectarian exclusion: *In the absence of relational unity, our convictions and preferences are sufficient to justify harsh judgments about the legitimacy of another's faith in Christ Jesus.*

Doctrinal heresy is to deny either the deity or humanity of Jesus. It is to abandon the need for or ground of salvation. It is to repudiate the sufficiency of Christ's death and resurrection for human redemption. It is to demolish and flatten the gospel message of redemption through Jesus Christ. The desire to maintain the unity of the church must never be an excuse for tolerating such points of view. But these are not the issues that have divided the body of Christ across the history of the church. Should we divide the church over conflicting understandings of "this is my body" and "this is my blood" in the Lord's Supper? Should we go separate ways over the interpretation of spiritual gifts and their ongoing place in the body? Should we cut off from fellowship all who disagree with us over the appropriate age for baptism or the verbal formula to say over the act?

The chasm is pretty wide between Protestants and Catholics, but I had an experience a few days ago that was instructive to me. I went to the airport and made my way through security. Because there would be no food on my noon flight, I went to a sandwich shop to get a quick bite to eat. I ordered, got my food, and paid. But there were no tables free. So I stood and waited for a couple of minutes. A lady finished her meal and bussed her table as she was leaving. I moved toward it, only to be met by another sandwich-on-tray soul in search of a place to eat it.

As I looked at the man, I smiled and asked, "Are you of a spirit to share this table with another hungry soul?" "Of course," he said. So we sat down. We put our trays on the table, shook hands, and introduced ourselves. "Would you be willing to offer thanks for our food?" I asked.

By the way, I suppose I ought to let you know that I don't typically ask total strangers to pray with me at airports. But he was wearing a clerical collar, and I assumed—correctly as it turned out—that he was a Roman Catholic priest. Father Ken said he would be pleased to bless our food. Then, after making the sign of the cross, he thanked God for his gracious provisions and asked him to bless us in our travels.

In the course of the conversation that followed, he told me he was originally from Mississippi and was now serving a church in North Carolina. "Did you have many Baptist or Church of Christ friends back in Mississippi?" I asked him. "Any that you ate or prayed with?" He said he had had none, and we talked about the reasons why. I halfway apologized for engaging him in a conversation so theological at our first meeting and chance luncheon together. But I explained that I was bothered by the fact that there was so much division and sectarian rivalry among people who claim to be Christians. I told him that a friend and I were writing a book about unity and that our point would be that relational unity with Christ was the key to unity with one another—not institutions, church organization, or creeds outside Scripture.

He was thinking as he took a bite. Then he looked me in the eye and said, "That's how I had to deal with the racism of my youth. The civil rights movement didn't change me. Even my knowledge that racism is wrong didn't change me. I got to know some African-American people, and that is when I changed. A real relationship with real people who were different from me taught me to get past my prejudice." We agreed that a new day had dawned for the possibility of building relationships with people whose practice of the Christian faith is not uniform—and exchanged names and addresses so we could continue our contact.

While working in Egypt for several months, my friend who was there to help with medical training found that labels and distinctions that might have kept Christians apart in America were irrelevant. Worship on the Lord's Day, prayer, encouragement—these spiritual needs were addressed in the name of Jesus rather than in the name of their denomination. Living in a Muslim country where Christians have limited social privileges, denominational loyalties mean very little.

While serving in the United States Army in Afghanistan and Pakistan, another friend had similar experiences. He told me, for example, of finding a tiny group of believers in Pakistan. "The official name of Pakistan is the Islamic State of Pakistan, but about three percent of the people are Christians. In that little church I found, the Christians didn't argue about worship styles or whether you should allow someone who has been divorced to come to your church. Those people had to stick together just to survive. We had some Catholics there, some Baptists and Methodists. They don't even think about those denominational names. That was a lesson we could all take from them."

In his epistle to the church at Rome, Paul had to deal with some "weak" brothers who were advocating a no-meat (14:2), no-holiday/holy day (14:5), no-wine (14:21) position—and insisting that everyone else in that church embrace their understanding and practice. They passed harsh judgment on those who viewed any of those issues differently. The "strong" brothers could eat meat, celebrate holidays/holy days, and drink wine without offending their consciences. Frankly, it is a bit difficult to be sure where these points of view originated. Were the "weak" Jewish believers who were offended by the Greek majority? Were they Gentile Christians whose philosophies led them to extreme, ascetic postures? We cannot be certain.

Whatever the origin of their points of view, the problem is clear. *Both* groups were wrong and were sinning against each other. The weak had tended toward legalism, judgment, and condemnation; the strong had tended toward superiority, judgment, and condemnation.

The doctrinal position held by either group was tolerable to Paul. But the attitude displayed by both groups was *not* tolerable. The apostle was grieved that harsh feelings over these non-fundamental issues were causing a rift in the church. So he reminded them that Jesus is Lord over all believers (14:9) and told them that they had no right to sit in judgment on each other (14:10-11).

These same issues are still matters of strong conviction among people in local churches and whole denominations. We don't have many who press for vegetarianism. But I can take you to some who argue vehemently about the appropriateness of Christians observing Passover, Christmas, or Earth Day. And I guarantee that I can cause a church fight in practically any church by putting the question "Can a Christian drink alcoholic beverages?" on the floor. And the disputants will not be content to say their points of view are "mere matters of opinion." Each side will appeal to the Bible and believe sincerely that its case is right and the other's wrong.

Maybe hearing these verses from a fresh, contemporary paraphrase will make them more emphatic to us:

> Welcome with open arms fellow believers who don't see things the way you do. And don't jump all over them every time they do or say something you don't agree with—even when it seems that they are strong on opinions but weak in the faith department. Remember, they have their own history to deal with. Treat them gently....
>
> None of us are permitted to insist on our own way in these matters. It's God we are answerable to—all the way from life to death and everything in between—not each other. That's why Jesus lived and died and then lived again: so that he could be our Master across the entire range of life and death, and free us from the petty tyrannies of each other.
>
> So where does that leave you when you criticize a brother? And where does that leave you when you condescend to a sister? I'd say it leaves you looking pretty silly—or worse. Eventually, we're all going to end up kneeling side by side in the place of judgment, facing God. Your critical and condescending ways aren't going to improve your position there one bit....
>
> Cultivate your own relationship with God, but don't impose it on others. You're fortunate if your behavior and your belief are coherent. But if you're not sure, if you notice that you are acting in ways inconsistent with what you believe—some days trying to impose your opinions on others, other days just trying to please them—then you know that

you're out of line. If the way you live isn't consistent
with what you believe, then it's wrong....
    So reach out and welcome one another to God's
glory. Jesus did it; now you do it! (Rom. 14:1,7-10,22-
23; 15:7, *The Message*).[6]

No, we may never have the same name, polity, and worship
practices. We may never work out all of our doctrinal differences on lifestyle expectations. And we may never achieve
institutional unity. But that was never heaven's intention for
us. The unchurched world does not judge us by our organization and doctrines but by our demonstration of Christian
love for one another. If we cannot love each other in Christ,
how can we expect the world to believe our testimony about
him? As long as we are hostile to one another, isn't it likely
that more and more of the unsaved world will be hostile to
us all?

    What biblical text helps us discern the *relational anchor
point* for believers concerned about unity? Surely we could
find no greater challenge than the words of Jesus: "I give you
a new commandment, that you love one another. Just as I
have loved you, you also should love one another. By this
everyone will know that you are my disciples, if you have
love for one another" (John 13:34-35).

Missional Issues

    The most obvious way for Christians who want to
demonstrate their relational unity with one another to get
about the task is by joining hands for certain acts of ministry
that are common to all who are trying to follow Jesus. These
acts in support of Christ's mission to the world are deeds of
observable love to a watching world.

Think about it: Did Jesus conduct seminars in biblical doctrine or exhort his followers to upright, loving, and compassionate treatment of their fellow human beings? The answer to that question is too clear to debate, right?

Think about it: When his critics pressed controversial issues of biblical interpretation on Jesus, what was his reaction? Sometimes he pushed them about their motives in posing the question (cf. Luke 7:36-50). Sometimes he pointed beyond their quibbling to the greater obligation of compassion (cf. Luke 13:10-16). And sometimes he just told one or more of his cryptic stories and left them to wonder about its significance to the question at hand (cf. Luke 15:2ff). I don't recall a single instance where he indicated he thought the question was nearly as important as they were making it out to be.

> *When faith is completely replaced by creed, worship by discipline, love by habit; when the crisis of today is ignored because of the splendor of the past; when faith becomes an heirloom rather than a living fountain; when religion speaks only in the name of authority rather than with the voice of compassion, its message becomes meaningless.*
>
> –Abraham J. Heschel

Jesus defined his own mission in the world by his reading of an Old Testament text in the Nazareth synagogue. It is of some interest in retrospect that he did not take up the prophecies of Isaiah 7, 9, or 53. Neither did he take up the

several texts that tied the Messiah to King David. Instead he
read from Isaiah 61:

> Then Jesus, filled with the power of the Spirit,
> returned to Galilee, and a report about him spread
> through all the surrounding country. He began to teach
> in their synagogues and was praised by everyone.
>
> When he came to Nazareth, where he had been
> brought up, he went to the synagogue on the sabbath
> day, as was his custom. He stood up to read, and the
> scroll of the prophet Isaiah was given to him. He
> unrolled the scroll and found the place where it was
> written:
>
> "The Spirit of the Lord is upon me,
>   because he has anointed me
>   to bring good news to the poor.
> He has sent me to proclaim
>   release to the captives and
>   recovery of sight to the blind,
>   to let the oppressed go free,
>   to proclaim the year of the Lord's favor."
>
> And he rolled up the scroll, gave it back to the
> attendant, and sat down. The eyes of all in the syna-
> gogue were fixed on him. Then he began to say to
> them, "Today this scripture has been fulfilled in your
> hearing." (Luke 4:14-21)

He showed us the meaning of a life under the kingdom
rule of God. He alone can save. All his disciples can imitate
his concern for the poor, persons in prison, the blind, and
those weighed down by life's heavy burdens. We can follow

his example of righteousness, compassion, and love. Just as the kingdom of God broke onto the human scene through his kindness to those in need and his acceptance of the outcasts, so does the presence of the kingdom become known today when those who wear his name act in his name to do the same. While these ministries may well pave the way for the hearing of the gospel, caring about and serving people needs no greater justification than that such behavior continues the mission of Jesus.

In August of 1992, Hurricane Andrew hit Florida with devastating force. It caused an estimated $25 billion in economic devastation, made thousands homeless, and killed some forty people. Fourteen tractor-trailers and three C-130 cargo planes were sent from Nashville to various places of critical needs. The primary collection sites were situated on properties of a Baptist Church, Pentecostal Church, Presbyterian Church, Methodist Church, and Church of Christ. Secondary sites were on other church properties across Middle Tennessee. The reason so much was done so quickly in that situation is that these churches decided God would be honored and more help delivered if we worked together instead of separately. Local television, radio, and newspaper supported the project without reservation precisely because it was inter-denominational and utterly non-sectarian. It was out of character for Nashville churches!

Since then we have worked together to send tens of thousands of dollars worth of medical relief to a children's hospital in Moscow, help rebuild eight church structures that were burned mysteriously in 1996, and sponsor the Middle Tennessee Billy Graham Crusade in 2000. In the meanwhile, we have worked together on dozens of less visible projects to help the sick, unemployed, drug-addicted, and homeless of our city.

These are missional ties among churches that have found common ground in Christ. Compassion for hurting people is the common language of African-American, Caucasian, and Latino believers in our city. And while we have beliefs too distinctive to sponsor joint prophecy conferences or seminars on spiritual gifts, we share the core belief in Jesus Christ as Savior that allows us to join as one to preach the gospel.

The thesis of this book that the uniting power of Jesus is greater than the divisive power that has been at work for so long is demonstrable. If it can take place in the heart of the Bible Belt where social, racial, and religious tribalism have run rampant so long, it can take place anywhere.

So, finally, is there a biblical text that specifies the *missional anchor* point for believers who want to maintain Christian unity? Perhaps it is found in the writings of Paul: "So then, whenever we have an opportunity, let us work for the good of all, and especially for those of the family of faith" (Gal. 6:10).

Jesus: Our Benchmark

I can envision a variety of denominations being needed for the evangelism of the twenty-first century world. Some will be reached by communities of faith that value ritual more than others. These churches may use robes, candles, and eucharist as means for reaching out with the gospel. Others will be touched by informality in which music is the primary literature. All will demand some degree of life engagement that is authentic, affirming, and supportive. They will need places of acceptance, healing, and opportunity for service to others.

Sectarianism is not likely to have as many possibilities in our Postmodern culture as it was able to exploit in the past hundred years or so. It is to denominational Christianity what "unrecoverable" is to a computer crash or "fatal" is to a heart attack. It is a judgmental and divisive spirit that will tolerate neither mystery nor differences. People infected with it assume they and their group are right about everything. They uphold everything their group does and for which it stands. They oppose everything and everybody in a different camp.

Isolation and judgmentalism are *not* doctrinally sound within the Christian faith. They are at the heart of a sectarian spirit. And that spirit is hateful to Christ and should be abhorrent to his followers as well.

For one thing, a sectarian spirit is arrogant. His choice of a denomination fixes his position on practically every issue. Her church membership makes thinking unnecessary—even undesirable. After all, other groups are seen by him as wrong on everything. They couldn't possibly be right—or they'd see everything the way she does.

"But we can't *all* be right on predestination, church organization, the Lord's Supper, and dozens of other important issues!" someone objects. "We need to be honest enough to tell the people who are wrong about those things that they're not right with God and therefore we can't fellowship them."

Of course we aren't *all* right. *We're all wrong!* Oh, we're not all wrong about everything. But all of us have our blind spots—created by everything from ethnocentrism to sloppy scholarship to honest error. Salvation is neither by good works of moral behavior nor the good work of doctrinal perfectionism. It is through a relationship with Jesus that is created by a birth from above. The truth we must "know" and by whom alone we may be "made free" is personal rather than syllogistic, Jesus himself rather than a set of doctrines about him.

Sectarianism defies the teaching of Christ. He confronted the sectarian spirit of his disciples one day as they reported (with apparent satisfaction) that they had tried to stop a man from casting out demons "because he was not following us." This was his response: "Do not stop him; for no one who does a deed of power in my name will be able soon afterward to speak evil of me. Whoever is not against us is for us" (Mark 9:38-40).

> *Doubt is part of the arsenal of faith. It keeps it fresh and honest. In our daring to argue and in our struggle to understand, the blood begins to flow through a tired and worn-out faith.*
>
> –Alan W. Jones

"But if the Baptist (Pentecostal, Nazarene, etc.) Church is saving souls, every other denomination should just take down their sign and join them!" protests another. "If they're doing the job right— especially if they're making more converts than we are—then we have no justification for our existence." In some settings, that is probably correct. And it is only sectarian pride that demands that one group "move in on" and "compete with" a given group of Bible-believing, Christ-honoring souls rather than join with and encourage them.

In the majority of cases, however, it likely is *not* best to try to fit every heart into one cluster of believers. Back to a point already made about the potential value of a variety of denominations, there are just too many differences in temperament, outlook, and taste to permit it—without the sort of coercion that has been attempted again and again across Christian history. "One size fits all" may be a practical idea with cheap socks, but not with anything really important and in which people invest their lives and destinies. Sectarianism confuses the task and mission of the church. Churches—whether Baptist, Churches of Christ, Presbyterian, or Pentecostal—are not arbiters of truth, and those of us who are members of churches are not commissioned of God to judge one another. To the contrary, there is an apostolic word to us: "Why do you pass judgment on your brother or sister? Or you, why do you despise your brother or sister? For we will all stand before the judgment seat of God" (Rom. 14:10).

"But where does it stop?" screams a passionate soul. It certainly stops at Jesus. If we confess his own claims, we must confess him to be the Way, Truth, and Life who alone provides access to the Father (John 14:6). The one thing about which one cannot be wrong and still be a Christian is Jesus Christ. Surely there will be people in heaven who have been wrong about *everything* else. Indeed, if that is not the case, how could I ever be sure that the essential list of necessary items about which one must be infallibly correct is mine? Or do I embrace yours? Or do we both abandon the search in neurotic exhaustion? I know people who have done just that out of a variety of backgrounds because they had believed the lie of sectarianism.

All Bible-believing churches are in danger of being sectarian. Members of denominations and non-denominations alike have been guilty of it at one time or another, to one degree or another, to one level of harm or another.

As a friend observed recently, there seems to be a refreshing move of the Holy Spirit in many quarters that brings encouragement to everyone—everyone, that is, except those who are sectarian. Community Bible Study and Women's/Men's Bible Fellowship Groups are drawing hundreds of thousands together for a fresh reading of the Word of God. Promise Keepers, the Billy Graham Crusades, and many similar efforts provide people who have known each other only in caricature the chance to know how sincere the passion for Christ really is in the larger body of Christ. These are things for which we surely ought to be praising God rather than growing defensive.

Maybe the time is coming when we can be mature enough to admit our limited grasp of the biblical data without feeling compromised. Strong convictions don't have to be borne with an ugly, hypercritical attitude toward others. One should feel no embarrassment about changing his mind on something. Strong convictions held with integrity allow one the option of learning more. Unyielding dogmatism forces one to run from truth for the sake of defending a position already taken. *Humility* is a Christian virtue.

The benchmark is Jesus Christ, not Churches of Christ. It is Jesus Christ, not the Lutheran Church. It is Jesus Christ, not the Roman Catholic Church. It is Jesus Christ. Not tradition. It is Jesus Christ. Not the Bible as translated by a certain person or group or as interpreted by a given hermeneutic, trained exegete, or polemic champion. *Jesus Christ!*

Conclusion

Honest inquiry in seeking after Christ is wholesome. It fosters modesty. And it protects us from the conceit that makes our collective rhetoric about the gospel insufferable to a watching world that has rejected religion while embracing spirituality. What two writers have called "the Jesus proposal" in this book is simply a plea for honest souls to seek Christ with humility. Be less concerned about right answers than right relationships. Worry less about systems than loving God and loving your neighbor as yourself.

In whatever denomination or non-denomination any one of us may be, seek Jesus above all. If you are not affiliated with any group of believers, we can only plead with you to find a Jesus-intoxicated group within which you can flourish. Just as you learn basketball, sculpting, or surgery best by being an apprentice among people who already practice it well, so will you learn to be a Christian most naturally among others committed to the same goal. Please don't forfeit the experience of healthy community because of the painful and embarrassing examples of a dysfunctional church whose failures you know.

It may not be the church you grew up in or where you first learned the gospel. It may not be the church where you are now. But it needs to be a group of people who understand the relational unity of the body of Christ and who are committed to living that unity with one another and with Christians of other traditions both theologically and missionally. It needs to be a fellowship that values its unity in Christ too much to commit idolatry by elevating some distinctive of its own to a status worth splintering his spiritual body.

Thinking back to the beginning of this chapter, a final optimistic note can be sounded. Yes, Postmodern men and women can think in terms of "spiritual but not religious" and avoid the church for the sake of its schisms and mutual judgments. One of the most hopeful strategies for drawing them to the church would be for it to value, pursue, and preserve unity among believers. One of their most solid values is *community*, and there is no community so appealing as one that lives to honor God through Jesus Christ, one that is filled by the Holy Spirit. The New Testament makes it clear that the church is designed to be a beautiful community of redemptive love. And who wouldn't want to share in a community such as that?

We are hardly in position to give a clear and unambiguous vision of how the Jesus project would look when implemented. After all, we have never seen or participated in its complete realization. We certainly cannot create it, for that is the work of the Holy Spirit. But the issues raised here seem crucial. If we cannot anchor ourselves in Christ and to one another in these three minimal ways, it seems doubtful that the oneness we long for will be anything more than a wistful yearning destined to remain unfulfilled.

Notes

1. "Charting unchurched America," *USA Today*, March 7, 2002, p. 1D.

2. " 'Amen' to a church-free life," *USA Today*, March 7, 2002, p. 7D.

3. "Will religion survive?" *USA Today*, March 27, 2001, p. 1B; available online at http://www.usatoday.com/educate/college/healthscience/casestudies/20020313-religion.pdf.

4. Unless this is the single exception in Acts, the terms "disciple" (Gk, *mathetes*) and "Christian" are interchangeable (cf. 11:26). These disciples are also said to have "believed" (NIV) or to have been "believers" (NRSV) prior to Paul's arrival. Cf. F. F. Bruce, *Commentary on the Book of the Acts* (Grand Rapids: Wm. B. Eerdmans, 1954), pp. 385-386.

5. This would most naturally refer to church life in different historical periods (e.g., racist policies of church membership and life in 1830 as opposed to 1980). But it would also include the significant differences that exist simultaneously among Churches of Christ in different regions of the United States, in various countries of the world, or within different ethnic settings.

6. Eugene Peterson, *The Message: The New Testament in Contemporary Language* (Colorado Springs: NavPress, 1993).

We must beware lest we
violate the holy, lest our
dogmas overthink the mystery,
lest our psalms sing it away.
The right of interpretation
is given only to one who
covers his face, "afraid to look
at God," to one who,
when the vision is forced
upon him, says:
"I am undone . . .
for mine eyes have
seen the King."
We can only drink the flow
of thoughts out of the
rock of their words.

–Abraham J. Heschel

9. SO JUST WHO IS MY SISTER/BROTHER?

Rubel Shelly

More than a dozen years ago now, I had a conversation with a lady that has been duplicated by both John and me in a variety of other settings. She had never attended an assembly of our church. The conversation took place at the suggestion of a mutual friend who assured her it would be a safe context for honest study of the questions that were bothering her. Here is how the discussion went.

"Mr. Shelly, I have been studying the subject of baptism for about two years now," she began. "I'm in a real dilemma at this point and don't know what to do about it. I'm really hoping you can . . ." Her voice trailed off, and tears began to come down both cheeks and choked off any further words for a moment. So I took the lead for a couple of minutes just to let her catch her breath and compose herself.

"This is obviously very important to you—and very emotional. Since I don't know you and have no basis for understanding the struggle, I probably need you to give me a little background," I said to her. "Could you begin perhaps by telling me something of your spiritual journey? Are you wrestling with the gospel story and deciding about accepting Christ? Or have you already been baptized—and has something happened to undermine your sense of security in Christ?" She had wiped her eyes by then and taken several deep breaths. "I'm all right now," she said. "Maybe I should give you a quick summary of my life. I promise not to give you all the boring details! But it might help you appreciate my question.

"I'm 34 years old and am the organist for a Methodist Church not far from here. I grew up in a Christian home, and my parents are the godliest people I've ever known. (She dabbed her eyes and almost choked down again at the mention of her mother and father.) They have always been there for me, and my mother is the favorite and best Sunday School teacher I've ever had.

"I've been working on my master's degree in sacred music for almost two years now—I told you I'm organist for a church, didn't I? Well, I took an elective course in New Testament theology my very first semester in seminary and was fascinated by several of the things I learned from the lectures and readings. But the topic that piqued my interest the most was baptism. To be honest, I had never realized that immersion was the original mode for it or that infant baptism isn't documented before the late second century. And that set me thinking about my own experience as a Christian.

"My parents had me baptized when I was just a few weeks old—I don't know exactly. I don't remember it, of course. And I think that's a big part of my problem now! I'm wondering if I should be baptized again—by immersion this time. I would like to do it as an act of personal witness to my faith. I would like to have an event that I do remember—an event I chose for myself. Am I making any sense?

"But here's the problem with doing what I'm thinking about (and she began to cry again!): I can't repudiate my parents. I can't do something that they could see as my 'judgment' or 'condemnation' of them. And I really do believe that I am already a Christian who has tried to serve Jesus with my life.

"Mr. Shelly, do you regard me as a Christian? Do you count me your sister in Christ? Or do you think I am lost and need to be saved?"

So What Would *You* Say?

Before telling you what I say to people in those settings, tell me what you would say. Just pause a minute, put this book down, and visualize such a person talking with you. Answer the three questions she put to me before reading on.

On the assumption that you took the challenge to answer the lady's three very specific and pointed questions, what do you think you would have said to her? I hope you weren't too glib or quick with your response. Whether you answered "yes" or "no" to her, I hope you grasped the need to be both sensitive to her tender heart and faithful to Holy Scripture. Of course, you could just evade the questions by saying we human beings can't decide what another person should believe. You could say that we can't decide someone else's destiny. That would be true, of course, but it wouldn't be very helpful. She didn't ask me to tell her what to believe. And she didn't ask me to judge her—any more than she was willing to be asked to sit in judgment on her parents. People who ask questions like these aren't asking us to do God's work of judging the world. They're just looking for our best insights into how to deal with the struggles of their spiritual lives. That is a trust not to be taken lightly! For what it may be worth to you, here is what I say to questioners such as that lady.

"Of course I see you as a Christian! And I'm sorry you have apparently met somebody from a Church of Christ or some other immersionist group who treated you otherwise. Please judge me only for myself, all right? I understand the word 'Christian' to mean 'one who is following Christ' or 'one who gives allegiance to Christ.' And what you have just told me fairly screams your desire to honor him and do his will. While you and I probably won't see eye-to-eye on everything about the Christian religion—I can't even claim that for my wife and me—we certainly *do* see our faith in and love for Jesus to be at the heart of our identities.

> *Truth rests with God alone, and a little bit with me.*
>
> –Yiddish Proverb

"So, yes, I see the two of us as equals and peers. We are brother and sister to each other in the one great family or church of the Living God. We are sometimes-confused and always-inadequate believers who are trying to grow in our faith. We are both Christ-followers who want to be closer to the one we confess as our Lord.

"And, no, I don't think you are lost. You are no 'unbeliever' or 'pagan' in my eyes. For someone such as me who believes a Christian can fall away from grace and be lost, let me be clear: I don't think that happens when a believer has a flaw in her theology or character. I believe people in Christ can be lost if they deliberately reject the truth and willfully sin against God. But for his grace to his children in our frailty, misinterpretations, and sins, not even one of us could have the hope of salvation."

Coded Language and Confused Thinking

Every denomination and non-denomination has its distinguishing code language and in-house jargon. A Pentecostal brother will want to know if such-and-such person is "Spirit-filled"; the term means something different to him than it would for a Baptist. On the other hand, a sister from Baptist or Church of Christ background might ask, "Has so-and-so been baptized?"; her answer will be narrower than someone responding from a Presbyterian or Methodist background. All I am illustrating is the obvious fact that terms like "Spirit-filled" and "baptism" signify different things to people whose religious vocabulary has been formed not simply from the New Testament but from particular religious traditions.

Those of us who have grown up in or spent several years within the Disciples of Christ, Christian Churches, and/or Churches of Christ—the three major groups affiliated with what is known as the American Restoration Movement—certainly do have a distinctive vocabulary. When we use the expression "plan of salvation," for example, we are employing a shorthand for our version of evangelicalism's "four spiritual laws." Ours is a variant of Walter Scott's five-finger exercise and—depending on the region of the country—indicates the following five steps: hear, believe, repent, confess, and be baptized or believe, repent, confess, be baptized, and live faithfully unto death.

One of the words that has been prominent in our discussions aimed at self-understanding is "brotherhood" or "fellowship." When we pray for God's blessings on "the brotherhood," whom are we including—or excluding? When we inquire about a prevailing point of view on this or that subject "in our brotherhood," what do we mean? If we use the word as a noun and speak of "our fellowship," don't we typically mean to embrace only those most like ourselves—and not the Baptists, Methodists, and Pentecostals? If we use it as a verb to talk about "fellowshipping" John Doe, what does that mean?

From Broader to Narrower Definitions

In the earlier days of our movement, there was a rather gracious and broad view of Christian fellowship that facilitated dialogue with individuals and groups trying to follow Jesus Christ in authentic faith. Thomas Campbell issued his famous *Declaration and Address* in 1809 "To all that love our Lord Jesus Christ, in sincerity, throughout all the Churches" and to "our brethren of all denominations." Alexander Campbell preached for Baptists and Presbyterians and affirmed them as his brothers and sisters in Christ. After he had represented a group of denominations in defending the Christian faith in a debate with the infamous skeptic Robert Owen in April of 1829 in Cincinnati, he preached for the Methodist Church in that city on the following Lord's Day. Half a century later, David Lipscomb drove a buggy for Roman Catholic sisters to assist in treating the victims of a cholera epidemic in Nashville in 1873. He preached not only for both instrumental and *a cappella* churches among the Disciples/Churches of Christ but for Methodists and other denominations.

When I was 14, I preached for an annual Decoration Day event in West Tennessee that had been co-hosted for years by the local Pentecostal Church, Baptist Church, and Church of Christ. Because interdenominational worship events were no longer typical of our folks in the 1950s, I wasn't sure what to do with the original request that came to me for that event. Brothers Capshaw and Jacobs told me about the service and that it was "our year" to provide the speaker. When I asked my primary theological advisors (i.e., my father and mother) what I should do, they counseled me that I should never turn down an invitation to preach Jesus. So long as I was not asked or expected to say anything I did not believe, they said, I should consider it an honor to be asked to speak.

Between the early 1800s and the mid-1900s, something happened to that "gracious and broad view of Christian fellowship" that had distinguished the Campbells, Stone, Lipscomb, and others.[1] The heirs to their work became narrow and sectarian. In the early twentieth century—especially after 1930—there was increasing isolation. The rhetoric became harsh and strident. The humbler approach that had permitted men and women within this heritage to be generous of spirit to their sisters and brothers in various denominations degenerated into judgmentalism.

> *Many of [the Bible's] treasures are lost to those who bring to it only small questions. If we treat the Bible like a railway timetable and ask of it questions suited to such a document, we will get the response suited to our question.*
>
> –Alan W. Jones

"Christians only, not the only Christians" was an early motto for the American Restoration Movement. It was meant to affirm the possibility that one could be "just a Christian" without having his or her faith judged by a human creed or structure. The words were taken seriously. There would be no headquarters, no written creed, no official delegates to national meetings on policy, no formal leadership outside the local church—trappings which these forebears believed had generated needless sectarian divisions in the body of Christ.

Born and reared in this heritage, why would I have needed counsel about accepting a preaching opportunity on Decoration Day in 1958? I was raised in a general environment which taught that we alone were Christians and that people in "the denominations" were lost. Debates in the first half of the century had hardened "our views" on baptism, church organization, worship, and a dozen other issues. A point of view had been staked out that alone was deemed orthodox, and a preacher or local church varied from that single point of view at great peril. A preacher might be "quarantined" for his opinion and suffer the end of his career in the larger fellowship or in his local church—or both.[2] A similar fate would come to a local church that continued to permit such a person to teach or have significant leadership responsibility.[3]

By the midpoint of the twentieth century, several constituent groups within the Stone-Campbell Movement were not only refusing to have fellowship with believers in the Baptist, Methodist, or Presbyterian Churches but with one another as well. Sectarianism had not only emerged but had been taken to its logical extremes. If one can regard as a sister or brother only those who hold identical understandings

on an ever-expanding list of doctrines, the circle gets pro-
gressively smaller. Fellowship is now approval and endorsement, and there can be "no fellowship with the unfruitful
works of darkness"; to the contrary, the only relationship one
can have with those with whom he disagrees is to "reprove
them." These words from the KJV rendering of Ephesians
5:11 do not envision refusing fellowship to other Christians.
They distinguish the world of pagan idolatry from the sphere
of "light" Paul's readers have found in Christ and challenge
believers to stay clear of the darkness they once embraced
apart from him. The use of such language to excoriate one's
fellow-pilgrims in the Lord is hardly consistent with the same
apostle's instruction in Romans 14 and elsewhere.

By the midpoint of the twentieth century, very little of the
original genius of the American Restoration Movement
remained. An irenic spirit had given way to a dogmatic posture. No longer even using the slogan "Christians only, but not
the only Christians," we were not searching for greater clarity
in the faith but were altogether defensive of our interpretations as being identical with the "one faith" of Ephesians 4.[4]
We did not present ourselves as Christians seeking to restore
the simplicity of the earliest church but claimed to be the perfectly restored church.

Salvation: Both *Process* and *Event*

We have suggested at an earlier point in this book that
spiritual fellowship should be extended to those who evidence
what might be called nothing more than a bare minimum of
personal faith in Jesus Christ. After all, how much does a person have to know in order to be saved? How clearly must
what she knows be *correctly interpreted* for salvation? What

evidences of *faith* must a person exhibit in order to be saved? How well-formed must his *character* be as a babe in Christ in order to be saved? These are important questions, but how shall we answer them without being presumptuous and judgmental? Equally important, how shall we answer them without compromising our own best understandings and convictions?

Perhaps we could clear the major hurdle in wrestling with this issue if we could get clear on the fact that *salvation is best understood as a relationship that matures over time than as any single event.* Ultimately, we are not to choose between event and process, of course, but to affirm both. Faith that is relational in nature can do that. For example, is my marriage "event" or "process"? Yes! There are distinct events such as our first date, my proposal and her acceptance, a ceremony, the birth of three children, the death of my wife's father, our daughter's hospitalization—each of these and many more are moments in time that have contributed to our getting married and staying married. There is also the total experience of our relationship that has evolved over time and for which there are no discreet events to list so much as there has been learning, molding, taking, giving, and sharing to the point that we are affectionately and devotedly partnered for life.

> *I'm not sure God put us here to do everything "just right." If so, most of us are poorly equipped for perfection.*
>
> –Gene Zimmerman

Come to think of it, marriage is probably as good an illustration as I can offer as a metaphor for the *relational faith*

John and I have written about since the opening page of this book. I am not in love with "the noble and holy institution of marriage"; I am in love with Myra Shelly. That's the same idea I am trying to understand and apply in my spiritual life. I am not "embracing a set of prepositional truths"; I embrace Jesus Christ as my Savior and Lord. John is not "committed to this set of distinctive interpretations"; he is committed to the Holy God who had revealed himself in Jesus Messiah. And let us try to flesh out this claim with an issue that has been particularly important in our own history. How does fellowship relate to baptism? If any degree of spiritual fellowship precedes it, has baptism in Jesus' name been stripped of its significance?

Both of us stand in a mainstream of understanding that characterizes most people in Churches of Christ. We believe that baptism is a command from Jesus and the apostles to all who confess Jesus as their Lord. Insofar as we can tell, there is no such thing as an "unbaptized Christian" who figures into the biblical material about the church. The very term smacks of an oxymoron to New Testament vocabulary. People who have died to sin and want to live now in and for Christ need to be buried, and "we have been buried with him by baptism into death, so that, just as Christ was raised from the dead by the glory of the Father, so we too might walk in newness of life" (Rom. 6:4).

The New Testament has a variety of case studies in salvation that are unambiguous on the place of Jesus Christ to the process but leave room for honest debate on the role of baptism. In our eagerness to be sure that no commandment of the Lord and his apostles is overlooked, we have sometimes pressed as hard for baptism as for faith in Jesus—sometimes, perhaps, harder. We have left ourselves open to the charge of teaching baptismal regeneration (i.e., saving efficacy attaches to the act of water baptism itself) by some who have heard us press our case too far.

For everyone who has offered the thief on the cross as a case study of someone saved by faith apart from water baptism, we have had no problem affirming that Christ saved that penitent criminal. But we would hasten to point out that the 3,000 souls on Pentecost are better models for us than the thief. After all, Pentecost was the birthday of the church when the gospel began to be preached in fullness after Jesus' resurrection. And Peter told the people who asked what they should do to be saved, "Repent, and be baptized every one of you in the name of Jesus Christ so that your sins may be forgiven; and you will receive the gift of the Holy Spirit" (Acts 2:38).

Before we rush to the conclusion from this important example that baptism is always the time at which someone is saved, recall that the sequence of events was different when the gospel began to be preached to the Gentiles. When Peter finally began to grasp that God shows no partiality and that the gospel is for people of all races and ethnic groups, he went to Caesarea and preached about Jesus to a devout Roman centurion named Cornelius. He told the story of Jesus' life and ministry, death and resurrection. He explained:

"[Jesus] commanded us to preach to the people and to testify that he is the one ordained by God as judge of the living and the dead. All the prophets testify about him that everyone who believes in him receives forgiveness of sins through his name.

While Peter was still speaking, the Holy Spirit fell upon all who heard the word. The circumcised believers

who had come with Peter were astounded that the gift
of the Holy Spirit had been poured out even on the
Gentiles, for they heard them speaking in tongues and
extolling God. Then Peter said, "Can anyone withhold
the water for baptizing these people who have
received the Holy Spirit just as we have?" So he
ordered them to be baptized in the name of Jesus
Christ. Then they invited him to stay for several days.
(Acts 10:42-48)

It isn't exactly the same as on Pentecost Day, is it? In
Jerusalem, the people hearing the gospel were promised not
only the forgiveness of their sins but the Holy Spirit in connection with baptism in the name of Jesus; in Caesarea, people received the Holy Spirit and only afterwards were told
anything about being baptized. What we have called a
modernity mindset could go crazy trying to work out the correct sequence and formula for salvation here. Postmodern
people won't see the "problem" unless it is pointed out. They
are far more inclined to think in terms of process rather than
event. Their way of thinking and reading is more like that of
the New Testament documents than modernity's penchant
for blueprints.

We refuse to think that no intelligent and devout person
could possibly differ from us on the interpretation of texts
such as these. "But can all of you be *right* about your interpretation?" someone demands to know. *No, but we could all
be mistaken.* Our confidence is in God's mercy to all who seek
him and not in the correctness of our interpretive skills. We
believe in his grace and not in the perfection of our obedience
to his commandments. No one will be saved in rebellion and

unbelief, but all who are saved will be so in spite of the imperfection of both their faith and performance. If that is not the case, then no one can be saved.

The Question of Baptism

For people with a Church of Christ background like our own, the real conversation reconstructed at the start of this chapter is a tough challenge. We feel compelled to affirm a distinctive believe that the immersion of penitent believers constitutes baptism as we understand it to have been practiced and taught by the first-generation church of God. Yet we somehow sense it goes too far to "de-certify" the Christian status of the majority of those who have ever confessed Christ over twenty centuries.[5] The truth is, of course, that some would flatly and emphatically declare that anyone whose experience was that of an "unscriptural baptism" simply isn't a Christian. But think about that position very carefully before committing to it.

When personalities such as Thomas Campbell, Alexander Campbell, and Barton W. Stone launched a "second reformation" of the church, they believed the church of Christ already existed—just that it needed to be more biblical in certain of its forms and practices. One of those forms was baptism, and both Campbells were immersed by a Baptist evangelist when they became convicted that the immersion of adults upon a personal confession of faith in Christ was part of what they termed "the ancient order of things." I know of no evidence, however, that supports the view that either man looked back in horror over the thought that they had not even been Christians until that June day in 1812 when Matthias Luce immersed them. To the contrary, the younger Campbell would later write that a Christ-loving, Christ-confessing person who has not been immersed is "a babe in Christ" or "an imperfect Christian"[6]—not an unbeliever or non-Christian. Though he placed emphasis on the importance of immersion to a believer's experience, he appears to have regarded a transformed life as more fundamental evidence of a person's redemption from sin than baptism.[7]

Campbell wanted no part of the doctrine of baptismal regeneration some of his heirs adopted and taught. He explicitly stated that if forced to choose between someone sprinkled in infancy and one immersed as an adult, he would look to the spiritual-mindedness and Christ-like behavior of the two. And what if these traits were manifest in the former rather than the latter? He explicitly said his preference would be toward the former rather than the latter. "Did I act otherwise, I would be a pure sectarian," Campbell wrote, "a Pharisee among Christians."[8]

> *We are soaked to the skin in the death of Christ. Our union with Christ drips from us. We never "get over" this immersion; this drowning in Christ's death marks us daily; we trail wet footprints of this drenching wherever we go; we never dry off.*
>
> –Michael Jinkins

With all due respect, what Campbell or anyone else thought about the place of baptism isn't authoritative. Scripture must have priority over the conclusions drawn from it by either novice students or trained theologians. But shall either use the words of Holy Writ? One person's "unmistakable reading" of this text is set against another's "confident conclusion" from another—or perhaps the same one! In citing Scripture on this point, however, perhaps the first text of relevance is this one: "Let us no longer pass judgment on one another, but resolve instead never to put a stumbling block or hindrance in the way of another" (Rom.14:13).

The Lord's Supper

Then comes the matter of the Lord's Supper. Should we use wine or grape juice? Must the bread be unleavened or was that an incidental matter to our Lord's institution of this holy feast? Must we imitate Jesus' practice that night and serve the bread first? Always? Should we use a single container of wine or distribute the fruit of the vine in individual cups? Have separate prayers for the two elements or have one prayer and pass both simultaneously? Have the worshipers come to the bread and wine or distribute the elements among the worshipers? Details such as these are not of the essence of the event, yet each one has been known to generate serious problems among brothers and sisters in Christ.

Then there are other features of the Lord's Supper that have been debated among Christians. For example, although the Lord Jesus instituted it on a Thursday night, most Christians today hold that it is especially associated with Sunday—the day of the resurrection and the day on which the church was established. But does anyone have the right to restrict its observance to Sunday and to say that its celebration on another day of the week is sinful? The Bible itself makes no such declaration. By what right would we presume to do so?

There is the controversy over the frequency of communion. Scholars of all backgrounds agree that the textual and historical evidence point to regular weekly observance of the Lord's Supper by the earliest believers. Their plenary assemblies on Sunday were not principally for preaching and teaching but for the eating of the Lord's Supper (cf. Acts 20:7; 1 Cor.11:17-22). Again, however, one is hard pressed to make a case that one sins by monthly or quarterly observance of this communion rather than weekly participation. Where is the biblical precedent for such a judgment?

In the Middle Ages the communal and body-affirming event of the Lord's Supper was transformed into the personal and private Mass. That unfortunate move turned the Lord's Supper into a "power event" for the clergy. One person chose to give or deny the presence of Christ with an individual wafer set upon or withheld from another individual's tongue. The New Testament calls for self-examination, not other-examination in communion. "A man ought to examine himself before he eats of the bread and drinks of the cup," said Paul at 1 Corinthians 11:28. It is not my prerogative to decide to admit you to Christ's table, nor yours to exclude me. Again, Christ alone must be the judge of us all.

The church of the Middle Ages further denied the unity of the body of Christ that is affirmed in the Lord's Supper by separating "clergy" from "laity" in the altered and corrupted event. By reserving the cup to the clergy alone, the body of Christ was dis-membered rather than re-membered in communion.

One of the significant assertions of the Reformation was that the Lord's Supper was to be returned to its more inclusive, more biblical form. Communion would again be a time for self-examination at a communal meal before the Lord. As to frequency, both Calvin and Luther pleaded for the practice of regular weekly communion. Zwingli argued instead for quarterly celebration of the Lord's Supper, believing that the meal would become too commonplace and ultimately trivial if taken every week. Although I grant the legitimacy of Zwingli's fear, experience since the Reformation tends to argue the reverse—that churches observing communion less frequently tend to value it less.

Our own heritage places a high value on the Lord's Supper. Going even further than the Reformation Movement, its early leaders insisted that communion was not the possession of the clergy. They would not tolerate making it into a private Mass. Neither would they hear to the "examination of candidates" to decide who would come to the Lord's table. They protested the use of tokens that insured a closed communion (i.e., closed to all but those who had been examined, approved, and granted a physical token that gave admission to special communion services). They believed such "examinations" reserved the Lord's Supper to a local church's members only or to those of one's own denomination. It is

> *You have been baptized, but think not that you are straightaway a Christian. The flesh is touched with salt: what then if the mind remains unsalted? But if you are buried with Christ within, and already practice walking with him in newness of life, I acknowledge you as a Christian.*
>
> –Desiderius Erasmus

Christ's table to which we have been invited by grace, not our table to which we admit or from which we exclude one another.

The Role of Women

An issue about which many in our culture are more concerned than baptism or the Lord's Supper is the ministry options for females in the church. Catholics and Protestants, liberals and conservatives—everyone will have to address this issue. It is most unlikely that a unified answer will be given, so one of two things will have to happen: Either local churches and whole denominations will have to divide over yet another issue of dispute, or Christians will have to learn to live together lovingly with one another and respect a variety of views.

The Bible can hardly be used to argue against women ministering, using their God-given talents, speaking in Christian assemblies, administering church programs, singing (congregationally, small groups, or solo), reading Scripture, sharing information about church projects, testifying, teaching sub-groups of the church's membership (whether female, male, or mixed), writing articles or poems that will be used by males, or otherwise participating fully in the life of local churches. A church's failure to encourage the development of female talent and work robs it of countless blessings. That same failure results in buried talents that return no dividend to the owner who entrusted them to the church through its female membership.

Have you ever thought about some of our inconsistencies among Churches of Christ? Some churches have quarterly business meetings that "men of the congregation" are invited

to attend. Many congregations have policies in their educational programs that require male teachers for eleven-year-
old boys who have been baptized but permit women teachers for boys of the same age who have not been immersed.
(Does immersion really make a boy a man? Does it mean his
mother can no longer lead a family devotional for her children or lead a prayer with him present?)

We have never heard anyone object to women song writers but know many who would rise up in holy horror at the
thought of a woman song leader. We permit women to write
articles in every brotherhood journal I know but often pro-
hibit them from teaching a class with even one adult male in
the room. Then there are the unwritten laws someone made
against such roles as females serving as greeter-ushers or
women passing communion to a congregation. A woman is
apparently permitted to pass the bread from side to side on
the pew but not down the aisle. A church office in Middle
Tennessee received a phone call a while back from a nearby
preacher on Monday morning. "Am I correct that some
women passed the Lord's Supper there yesterday?" he asked
the church secretary who answered the phone—and who
told me about the call. "No, you are not," she said. "But that's
the *only* meal women don't serve at this church!"

A relatively small percentage of churches in our fellowship
will allow a woman to chair a "ministry committee." Surely you
will admit that it seems a little strange for the Women's Ministry
of a church to be chaired by a man. It has also seemed strange
across the years that a brother with a high school education or
who is a C.P.A. is tapped to lead the church's Bible School
Ministry as opposed to a godly sister with an Ed.D. who is a
school principal or county superintendent of education.

It seems to us that these and other incongruities have been created by a careless confusion of being visible and on one's feet in the assembly with being "in charge" or taking the leadership of the church away from males. Is a man selected to make announcements about the sick "in charge of" the church? Why, then, would a woman "usurp authority" if she made an announcement in the same assembly about an upcoming women's retreat?

And have you ever thought about the New Testament passages we tend to ignore when discussing the role of women in the church? In addition to Paul's frequently cited "Women should be silent in the churches" (1 Cor. 14:34a), there is his instruction earlier in the very same epistle that "any woman who prays or prophesies" should cover her head while doing so (1 Cor. 11:5). In the Old Testament tradition of Miriam (Ex.15:20), Deborah (Judg. 4:4), Huldah (2 Kings 22:14), and Noadiah (Neh. 6:14), the New Testament acknowledges Anna as a "prophet" (Luke 2:36). Both Priscilla and Aquila took the man Apollos into their home "and explained the Way of God to him more accurately" (Acts 18:26). The evangelist Philip had "four unmarried daughters who had the gift of prophecy" (Acts 21:9).

In closing his epistle to the Romans, Paul sent personal greetings to several people who had been "a great help" to him, and eight of them were women (Rom. 16:1-16). The first one named was the person who appears to have carried the epistle to Rome for him, "Phoebe, a deacon of the church in Cenchrea." Many biblical scholars believe there was a female order of deacons in the first century. Among those in our own heritage who have subscribed to this view are Alexander Campbell, Walter Scott, Moses Lard, and Robert Milligan.

In the personal ministry of Jesus, a Samaritan woman became an evangelist to her city: "Many Samaritans from that city believed in him because of the woman's testimony" (John 4:39)—and Jesus did not rebuke her for speaking publicly about him. His ministry seems to have been funded, at least in part, by generous women who sometimes traveled with him and the apostles (Luke 8:1-3).

Challenged by our culture to face these issues, we must look anew at the biblical material with priority on living out a relationship with God and one another. Our purpose is no more to settle this issue than the others already raised. It is, instead, to make the point that godly Christians draw different conclusions on important matters and need to be able to acknowledge one another as brothers and sisters in spite of those differences, treat one another with respect and love, and set an example before a watching world of how life is supposed to work in the family of God.

A Handy-Dandy Guide to Fellowship

The list of items that could be specified here is practically endless. Christians have been known to reject one another as fellow pilgrims over their differences in matters that outsiders would find laughable. We have refused to acknowledge our brothers and sisters because of interpretations that are more cherished than a fellow-believer—no, more cherished than Christ himself!

Guides of the following sort have circulated in various forms across the years and in practically all denominations. We have chosen to construct only a "short form" with a mere 25 items. Although it is being presented facetiously, its purpose is actually quite serious. If spiritual fellowship may be shared only among those with identical beliefs, it seems highly unlikely that any two believers can regard one another as fellow-members in the family of God. The matter becomes even more problematic if the total membership of a given local congregation—to say nothing of the churches in a given denomination—is considered. If regarding others as your brothers and sisters depends on commonly embraced tenets of faith, how large can any church be? And whose beliefs within the group will be used as the standard by which to judge the others?

> *To stand on one leg and prove God's existence is a very different thing from going down on one's knees and thanking him.*
>
> –Soren Kierkegaard

Here are the guidelines for this test. First, each individual must fill out his or her own survey without consultation or coaching. In completed form, it becomes that individual's personal guide to spiritual fellowship. Second, each item must have a minimum of two responses. Some may have as many as three. For example, your response might be as follows to items 2 and 21:

	Agree	Disagree	Irrelevant to salvation	Necessary to sal.	Necessary to fellowship
2. One Lord	x			x	x
21. Participation in "Promise Keepers"	x		x		

Third, you may regard as a brother or sister in Christ only those who have checked each box in the five categories of response just as you have.

	Agree	Disagree	Irrelevant to salvation	Necessary to sal.	Necessary to fellowship
1. One God the Father					
2. One Lord					
3. One Holy Spirit					
4. One faith					
5. One baptism					
6. One body					
7. One hope					
8. KJV as only correct translation					
9. Social use of alcohol					
10. Wearing fur and/or eating meat					
11. Membership in Masons					
12. Tongues-speaking					
13. Communion once per quarter					
14. Females leading prayer in public worship					
15. Christians suing one another					
16. A literal 1000-year reign of Jesus on Earth					
17. Final Judgment					
18. A church disciplining immoral members					
19. Christian participation in a Passover service					
20. Contemporary Christian music in public worship					
21. Participation in "Promise Keepers"					
22. A Christian taking a life as a soldier in a just war					
23. A Christian swearing under oath in civil court					
24. Female believers wearing bikinis on a public beach					
25. A Muslim leading a prayer for peace in a Christian assembly					

Although this survey has not been administered over a wide spectrum of Christians, we are assured enough of the beliefs of our friends and family to affirm this: We know of no one whose answers to these questions we would expect to be identical with our own. As a matter of fact, *the two of us don't even give identical answers on each line!* Can there be no spiritual fellowship between the two of us? Can we not be members of a local church in which people give answers with more variance than between our own?

Should each of us move to set up a church for those who will use his criteria for fellowship? And one final question: *Isn't the thought of using such a guide for determining whom to claim as a sister or brother in Christ ridiculous?*

"So how are we to make sense of Paul's apostolic order at 1 Corinthians 1:10?" someone asks. The verse says: "Now I appeal to you, brothers and sisters, by the name of our Lord Jesus Christ, that all of you be in agreement and that there be no divisions among you, but that you be united in the same mind and the same purpose." Aren't we supposed to "be in agreement" on the Holy Spirit and his gifts? On social drinking of alcohol? Aren't we obligated to "be united in the same mind and the same purpose" on communion? On female roles in the life of the church? On taking a life as a soldier? No, for the Apostle to the Gentiles didn't make that demand of his first-century readers; the same Spirit-guided apostle who wrote 1 Corinthians 1:10 also wrote Romans 14 and gave believers permission to hold contrary views on such subjects as these. In context, the agreement and unity the apostle demanded of Christians then and the Holy Spirit seeks among us today is unity of witness to the centrality, sufficiency, and saving power of the death of Jesus Christ (cf. 1 Cor.1:17-18; 2:1-5).

A Precedent to Guide Us

A King of Judah once took the initiative to call the Jewish people to observe the Passover. After the collapse of the Northern Kingdom in 722 B.C. and in connection with the cleansing of the temple at Jerusalem, King Hezekiah called people from both Judah and Israel to keep the Passover together as brothers in their Holy City. Although many turned a deaf ear to his invitation, thousands began moving toward Jerusalem. The covenant community would come together to celebrate its version of Independence Day, when Yahweh set their ancestors free from their Egyptian overlords by a mighty hand.

The Passover lambs were killed and the celebration began. Some from the northern areas arrived too late, however, to perform the required purification rituals that took several days for completion. So, although "a multitude of the people, many of them from Ephraim, Manasseh, Issachar, and Zebulun, had not cleansed themselves, yet they ate the passover otherwise than as prescribed" (2 Chron.30:18a). Or, as the New International Version renders the last words of this verse, "they ate the Passover *contrary to what was written.*" Would the rekindling of faith in Hezekiah's attempt at reformation be stopped in its tracks by their impurity and unauthorized eating of the sacred meal? Would God destroy those who had violated the Passover rules?

This is how the dramatic story ends: "But Hezekiah prayed for them, saying, 'The good Lord pardon all who set their hearts to seek God, the Lord the God of their ancestors, even though not in accordance with the sanctuary's rules of cleanness.' The Lord heard Hezekiah, and healed the people" (2 Chron.30:18b-20).

The violation of the purification laws in Hezekiah's day was not a matter of cavalier disobedience. The people were not defying God but seeking him. Precisely because the good king knew the difference between rebellion and the failure of those who "set their hearts to seek God," he had the generosity of spirit to pray for them to be accepted in their deficiency. And because God ultimately judges on the basis of a seeker's heart rather than his or her performance, he showed mercy, forgave their shortcomings, and healed them.

Could we lower some of the Satan-inspired and human-erected walls that divide Christians from one another? Perhaps live by a broader definition of fellowship within the family of God than some of us have experienced to date? Might we learn that we have misrepresented one another at times and exhibited a shoddy form of religious bigotry toward people whose understandings of Scripture are different from ours? Would it be worthwhile to abandon sectarian rivalry in order to "be in agreement" for presenting the gospel to the world? Would it make our witness to Jesus as Lord more powerful for us to be unified around his name? Maybe renounce litmus-test doctrines for the sake of lifting up Christ? Could we ever learn to be gracious enough to pray—and ask to have prayed for us!—the prayer of Good King Hezekiah for those who are flawed in certain interpretations and practices?

Conclusion

This chapter began with a story about a conversation with an organist for the Methodist Church and her dilemma over baptism. Perhaps you are curious as to how that conversation ended.

"The ultimate issue at stake here is not your baptism so much as your personal integrity, your peace of mind, and your ability to keep growing in your faith," I told her. "And the last thing you should see happening here is some form of 'repudiation' of your mom and dad. They acted in good faith with you and the Lord to dedicate you to him as a baby. It certainly appears they kept their promise! As an adult, you came in here telling me that those godly people are responsible for your strong faith in and desire to please Jesus.

"If you should reach the same conclusion I have about believers immersion, please think of it as growth in your faith rather than a rejection of your parents. And know for sure that it won't be the last step in your own 'pilgrim's progress' into the heart of your Father in Heaven. Whenever you are fortunate enough to learn something you did not know before, don't feel threatened but happy. When you have an insight about the will of God that is fresh and new, thank God for it. And don't stop learning, growing, and accepting whatever he wants to show you."

> *Amazing grace!*
> *How sweet the sound*
> *That saved a wretch like me!*
> *I once was lost,*
> *but now am found;*
> *Was blind,*
> *but now I see.*
>
> *—John Newton*

She said later that it was the comment about "growth steps" that helped her most. What she had seen and come to believe didn't replace what she already knew or mean rejection of the people who had taught it to her. Her good heart in accepting what she had been taught with sincerity and a good conscience is the same thing that let her continue to learn, grow, and climb to new heights in her faith.

She made the decision to be immersed—and brought her parents to witness the event. She explained what she was doing. I read some biblical texts appropriate to what was happening. And her parents affirmed her and rejoiced with her. It was a wonderful experience to share with them. It was the sort of mutual encouragement to study, authenticity, and obedience that can happen when believers treat one another with respect rather than condescension and judgment.

Notes

1. As an example of the change in spirit between the early- to mid-1900s, consider the fact that N.B. Hardeman would make this emphatic statement when preaching in the historic Ryman Auditorium as late as 1928: "I have never been so egoistic as to say that my brethren with whom I commune on the first day of the week are the only Christians on this earth. I have never said that in my life. I do make the claim that we are Christians only. But there is a vast difference between that expression and the one formerly made. But you might ask what my objective is. Exactly that which prompted and moved those [leaders of the American Restoration Movement, RS] of a century ago. I am trying to get all of God's people everywhere to stand together as a solid phalanx against the opposing forces now seeking to destroy the church of our Lord. I know that the cause of Christ needs it full strength. I know that in unity alone strength can exist, and I think it a calamity for those who claim to believe the Bible, to reverence Jehovah, and to wear the name of Christ at all, to stand thus divided, and thereby invite the enemy to a victory over our scattred forces." N.B. Hardeman, *Hardeman's Tabernacle Sermons*, Vol. 3 (Nashville: Gospel Advocate Co., 1928), p.125. By the final series of his "tabernacle sermons" at mid-century,

this language is notable for its absence both in Hardeman's preaching and in that of his peers.

2. Churches of Christ had no ordination to ministry beyond the local church. That was consistent with the view that presbyteries, conferences with voting delegates, and the like were unscriptural. To say that there was no method of being "defrocked" from ministry would be a mistake. A journal or school could effectively end a preacher's career by labeling him "unsound" on one or more hot-button issues such as premillennialism, church cooperation in evangelistic outreach, etc.

3. This would take such forms as the refusal of "sound" evangelists to schedule gospel meetings with that church or the loss of employment with a school or other parachurch entity for those who chose to continue as members of that body.

4. Whereas the New Testament typically uses the substantive term "the faith" as a reference to the central message about salvation in Christ (cf. Acts 6:7; 13:8; Gal.1:23; Phil.1:23, et al.), we came to use the term to embrace the totality of the New Testament corpus—as interpreted by a given champion who stood ready to defend doctrinal tangents with as much fervor as the deity of Jesus.

5. Many Christian groups practice infant baptism, and a significant majority of those who consider themselves Christians today have received "baptism" by the sprinkling or pouring of water in a religious ceremony rather than by total immersion. The Anabaptists were considered heretical for their adamant insistence on immersion. Anyone interested in seeing the basic arguments for each case could look up baptism in a multi-volume Bible dictionary. There will likely be one article written from each point of view.

6. Alexander Campbell, "Any Christians Among Protestant Parties," *Millennial Harbinger* (September 1837): 411; available online at http://www.bible.acu.edu/stone-campbell/Etexts/lun16.html.

7. "I cannot, therefore, make any one duty the standard of Christian state or character, not even immersion into the name of the Father, of the Son, and of the Holy Spirit.... It is the image of Christ the Christian looks for and loves; and this does not consist in being exact in a few items, but in general devotion to the whole truth as far as known." Ibid., p. 412.

8. Ibid.

Form together one choir,
so that, with the symphony
of your feelings and having
all taken the tone of God,
you may sing with one voice
to the Father through Jesus
Christ, that He may listen
to you and know you from
your chant as the canticle
of His only Son.

–Ignatius of Antioch

10. A CONCLUDING POSTSCRIPT

Rubel Shelly

Don't you sometimes get weary of hearing people talk about change? Don't you hate to see book titles about "transition" and "renewal"? And aren't you just worn out with the overuse of the term "reinventing"? Maybe our aversion to change can be explained.

We human beings tend, I fear, to be lazy. We prefer to float with the stream instead of choosing to swim against it. We ask for comfort instead of challenge. So we want to experience the unity of the body of Christ in a context of peace. No discomfort caused by being stretched. No conflicts borne of diversity and its inevitable disagreements. No talk of life in "an age of transition."

Change and Its Alternative

But change is the characteristic of life, and every living organism is undergoing constant alteration. Living things adapt to environmental changes. Things that don't respond to their environments with adaptations and transformations are dead—and may even become brittle fossils within their surroundings. Transition and change, then, should not be so frightening. They are signs of life. Rather than scare us, they should challenge the best within us. Instead of generating defensive resistance, they should be accepted as the necessary alternatives to death and decay.

These facts about plants and animals also can be applied to human beings, marriages, friendships, businesses, schools, and governments. And they relate as well to churches. That churches tend to value peace, sameness, and harmony is why so many of them are irrelevant, uninspiring, and dead. If you want peace in its ultimate form, go to a cemetery. If you want the life of Christ coursing through yourself, your fellows, and your surroundings, welcome the gospel—and brace yourself!

In the authentic community of the people of God, there is always conflict. As I heard Randy Harris put it once, life is different aboard cruise ships and battleships. The person in charge of the former has as a singular goal to keep everybody happy; the commander of the latter has the mission of equipping, training, and leading into combat. I cannot imagine the former as an appropriate metaphor for the people of God. Can you?

The thesis we have explored in *The Jesus Proposal* is that Christ's followers are called to model our faith in communities that exhibit unity in the midst of our diversity. More than that, we have argued that God is both pleased and honored in such a context. But, yes, most of us would have to change both our thinking and our behaviors in some significant ways in order to take such a thesis seriously. We tend naturally toward conformity rather than unity.

People are naturally more comfortable in settings where everyone looks, thinks, and acts alike. There is solace and predictability in uniformity. But the unity called for in the body of Christ is hardly to be equated with uniformity. As a matter of fact, the earliest church quickly learned that conformity rooted in demographic likeness is hardly God's idea of unity. They learned that, in fact, it is sinful.

Why do you think the original Christian community at Jerusalem was reluctant to include Samaritans? Why did those Christ-followers positively resist including Gentiles? Like us, they valued sameness. They had common history, Scripture, and lifestyle expectations. They lived pretty much alike—ate the same foods, spoke a common tongue, and viewed other cultures with suspicion. If the gospel were to be carried to other ethnic groups, things would get out of hand. And that scared those original believers whose "unity" was based on demography.

> *When our first parents were driven out of Paradise, Adam is believed to have remarked to Eve: "My dear, we live in an age of transition."*
>
> –William Ralph Inge

The Holy Spirit forced people such as Stephen, Philip, Peter, and Paul to cross demographic barriers and share the story of Jesus with Samaritans, Ethiopians, and the wider Mediterranean world. It created such incredible consternation that a conference of church leaders was convened at Jerusalem to debate the appropriateness of such actions. And I am certain that the underlying fear of the defenders of a status-quo, all-Jewish church was the traumatic change that would be ushered in by making the gospel equally available to all races. Can't you just hear that debate? "But everybody knows that people are happier and better off with people like themselves. Leave people to their own choices, and they will pick their own kind!" someone must have argued. "Why, we've never socialized or gone to school with those people. So why should we include them in our churches? They don't sing the way we do. They get so animated in their worship that it would scare our people to death. And we could never have another pot-luck dinner because we don't even eat the same foods. The very idea of disrupting the unity of the church of God over this sort of forced merging of races is unnatural. The next thing you know, our children will be dating one another—and marrying one another. And you can't make me believe there is any sane person here who wants that sort of outrageous thing to happen!"

I know the debate went something like that, for I listened to and ultimately participated in one just like it. I was born to a white Southern culture where meals, schools, and churches were uniform, not united. When I became convinced that demographic sameness was making a mockery of the gospel's call to unity in Christ and said so, I was fired—for the only time in my life, so far.

Spreading the gospel in diverse circumstances and to a variety of cultures creates new challenges. We have no clear precedents for handling them. We don't even have a common vocabulary with which to discuss them. Things quickly get out of our control. And, ah, that is the greatest fear of all. We don't like things "out of control"—our control. But if we do not believe the gospel is powerful enough to unite people of

great ethnic, cultural, and theological diversity, we are voic-
ing the fear that God can't handle what is beyond our ability to figure out. Shame on us!

Theological Diversity and Christian Unity

"But you just said the gospel creates unity among people
with 'theological diversity,' " someone says. "That's the part I
can't quite accept. Yes, it unites people of great ethnic and cultural difference, but it is agreement in our theology that creates unity that is greater than superficial differences of birth,
skin color, or language. The Bible asks: 'Can two walk together, except they be agreed?' And Paul wrote: 'Now I beseech
you, brethren, by the name of our Lord Jesus Christ, that ye all
speak the same thing, and that there be no divisions among
you; but that ye be perfectly joined together in the same mind
and in the same judgment.'"

Those are verses right out of the King James Version of the
Bible at Amos 3:3 and 1 Corinthians 1:10. The first one may
leave a false impression from that translation. The Hebrew text
more correctly translated asks this: "Do two walk together
unless they have made an appointment?" (NRSV). For the
moment, however, let's work with these verses in the familiar
language many of us know.

The question, "Can two walk together, except they be
agreed?" actually permits two very different answers. One
could answer negatively this way: "No, two people cannot
walk together *unless they are agreed on a direction for their
travel.*" She can't go north as he goes south—and be together.
But they can indeed walk together in the same general direction (e.g., football stadium, restaurant) and love one another
as friends or mates in spite of their disagreements (e.g., the

team for which to cheer, food of choice). One could answer positively this way: "Yes, two people who disagree can walk together *in order to discuss an important subject about which they differ.*" If we accept the better translation of the verse, it is not difficult to imagine that two people who respect each other have made an "appointment" precisely because they think the issue at hand (i.e., business, education, Christian doctrine) is important enough that it deserves to be thought through very carefully.

The parties in view at Amos 3:3 appear to be Yahweh and Israel, not two Hebrew prophets or theologians. No, God and his people could not walk together in the Negev except by agreement on their goal of a "land flowing with milk and honey." No, God and the people of Amos' time could not walk together in holiness and rebellion. Both in the wilderness experience and in the times of the prophets, Yahweh was always willing to walk with his confused and far-from-uniform-in-beliefs Chosen People by his compassion and grace—just as he does with his people still.

Paul was very concerned about the situation at Corinth. The Christians there were neither "speak[ing] the same thing" nor demonstrating that they were "perfectly joined together in the same mind and in the same judgment"; it could not be said that there were "no divisions among you" at Corinth. They were divided over preacher loyalty, and it had become such a sharp contention that they had turned it into a church quarrel. "What I mean is that each of you says, 'I belong to Paul,' or 'I belong to Apollos,' or 'I belong to Cephas,' or 'I belong to Christ.' Has Christ been divided? Was Paul crucified for you? Or were you baptized in the name of Paul?" (cf. 1 Cor. 1:10-17). What a spectacle that must have been for non-Christians who had come into their midst to learn the gospel—comparable to the experience some have today who wander into some Christian assemblies to find comfort after a horrible diagnosis or direction for their lives after a terrible moral failure, only to hear someone harangue Billy Graham or churches that don't identify the two beasts of the Apocalypse correctly!

About what did Paul want the church at Corinth to be in agreement? Everything? About what did he want them "united in the same mind and the same purpose"? All items of Christian doctrine and practice? Of course not, for it was this same apostle who insisted that believers give one another great latitude of conviction and action at Romans 14. Thus he would write: "Who are you to pass judgment on servants of another? It is before their own lord that they stand or fall. And they will be upheld, for the Lord is able to make them stand" (Rom. 14:4). The people of God at Corinth and Rome in the first century and at Presbyterian and Baptist churches today are to "speak the same thing" about the One who saves and sanctifies. Their best understandings of eschatology, church government, and Calvinism don't have to mesh. Their confession of Jesus Christ as the One alone who is Son of God and Lord of All must be the same.

What God Is Teaching Us About Unity in Christ

We believe that there was likely as much theological diversity in the first- and second-century churches as there is among Christian denominations today. At the very least, there was much more theological diversity in the original church than we have been willing generally to admit. The church in Acts and the Epistles had a theology that ran exceedingly deep but which was not very broad. They knew they believed in Jesus and wanted their lives to be surrendered to him. They confessed him as the Son of God. It took centuries of Christian history to develop creeds, theological formulations, and full-scale division of the church.

We believe that the unity of the Body of Christ in recent times has been rendered impossible because of the failure of Christians to distinguish the first-order truth of the gospel from less significant issues of denominational background, distinctive interpretations of biblical texts, and personal taste. It is the central story of Christ's death, burial, and resurrection for us that is "of first importance" (1 Cor.15:3ff). We have allowed lesser matters, even trivia, to distract us from what is genuinely central to Christianity.

> *Don't be so arrogant as to suppose that the truth is no bigger than your understanding of it.*
>
> –Michael Green

We believe that what Paul called "the unity of the Spirit" is indeed just that—a unity created by the Spirit-presence of God among those who confess Jesus as the Son of God. It is not our duty to create or devise an institutional framework for unity. We are simply called to acknowledge it, affirm it before unbelievers, seek ways to experience it for mutual encouragement and instruction with fellow-believers, and otherwise "make every effort to maintain the unity of the Spirit in the bond of peace" (Eph. 4:3). We believe that Paul pointed to the essential qualities that permit these things to happen when he called his readers to live "with all humility and gentleness, with patience, bearing with one another in love" (Eph. 4:2).

The world watched, held its collective breath, had its hopes ebb and flow, and prayed for nine coalminers who were trapped 240 feet underground in the Quecreek mine in Pennsylvania for three days in July 2002. On Wednesday night July 24, millions of gallons of water roared in on the men when their machinery punctured a long-abandoned mine. Old and outdated maps they were using had led them to think they were hundreds of feet from danger. Now they were trapped in a small, dark space—about four feet deep, twelve to eighteen feet wide—that was their safe place for seventy-seven hours.

The 55-degrees Fahrenheit water temperature threatened all of them with death by hypothermia. A trauma surgeon at the Memorial Medical Center in Johnstown, where six of the miners were hospitalized after their Sunday-morning rescue, said the miners "decided early on they were either going to live or die as a group." They tied themselves to one another. They talked and encouraged one another. "When one would get cold, the other eight would huddle around the person and warm that person," reported the physician, "and when another person got cold, the favor was returned."[1]

If Christians sensed the true peril we are in down here, we would huddle together just to keep one another alive. We certainly wouldn't be working against one another. And if the church ever learns how to be the church, it will be when we learn to love God by honoring and loving one another.

We believe that drawing near to God through Jesus Christ by means of such spiritual disciplines as prayer, worship, holy behavior, generosity, Spirit-empowered rejection of Satan-encouraged lusts, study of Scripture, and attention to the weakest among us is far different than modernity's penchant for drawing right conclusions on issues of theology—and far more important. The key to everything spiritual is new life in Christ, and that life of the Spirit is nurtured by drawing near to him in faith.

The hope for our survival in this world that has given its allegiance to the Prince of Darkness is not in ourselves but in the One whom John called "the true light, which enlightens everyone"—Jesus (cf. John 1:9). Yes, we tie ourselves together in love for safety. Yes, we share our meager provisions and strength. Yes, we huddle together in communities of faith to keep one another warm. But the work that can save us is being done up above. And we need yearning for God above fastidious scholarship. It is one thing to debate theology and quite another to trust God above all. The ultimate measure of our faith is not astute argument but obedience. The mission of our various churches is not to convince people of the distinctiveness of our version of Christianity but to lead men and women to be disciples of Jesus Christ.

When those nine men were trapped in a coalmine beneath the ground, their hope lay in what others were doing above them. A six-inch pipe had been sunk precisely into place to pump warm air to the miners. A drill big enough to extricate the men had to be brought in from West Virginia and took twenty hours to arrive. Once drilling had started, a 1,500-pound drill bit broke in hard rock about 100 feet down; there was another delay of eighteen hours. But the work continued by a determined crew of rescuers. In the meanwhile, what was the greatest need of the trapped miners? Scholars to produce a critical apparatus for the old maps—or faith to hang on? Did they need to debate their differences and move away from one another—or find reasons to cling to one another?

By the same token, heaven has all its resources at work constantly to rescue the lost. While we huddle in dark, cold places and confess our fears to one another, God is still at work. The Holy Spirit is active in us. The living Christ is seeing his redemptive work through to completion. "For if while we were enemies, we were reconciled to God through the death of his Son, much more surely, having been reconciled, will we be saved by his life" (Rom.5:10). In the meanwhile, we pray, "Our Lord, come!" In the meanwhile, we need to encourage one another to hang on for dear life. We need to cling to one another for hope. By the way, the first thing the rescued miners said was this: "What took you guys so long?" I suspect the purest of heart should anticipate saying something like that when Jesus eventually appears.

We believe that the clearest path to Christian unity is found not in conformity or doctrinal sameness but in a shared mission. The mission of the church is to declare that a new way for living that works both now and in a world yet to come has been exhibited and made possible for us through Jesus. Failing to understand that mission, the church has tended to make war on itself instead of fighting the real enemy.

Max Lucado tells about a fishing trip he made in high school with his father and a friend named Mark. After two or three days of bad weather that kept them in a camper and off the water, something happened to the wonderful dynamic that had been there when the trip began.

> When we awoke the next morning to the sound of
> sleet slapping the canvas, we didn't even pretend to be
> cheerful. We were flat-out grumpy. Mark became more
> of a jerk with each passing moment; I wondered what

spell of ignorance I must have been in when I invited him. Dad couldn't do anything right; I wondered
how someone so irritable could have such an even-
tempered son. We sat in misery the whole day, our
fishing equipment still unpacked.

The next day was even colder. "We're going
home" were my father's first words. No one objected.

I learned a hard lesson that week. Not about fishing, but about people. When those who are called to
fish don't fish, they fight.

When energy intended to be used outside is used
inside, the result is explosive. Instead of casting nets,
we cast stones. Instead of extending helping hands,
we point accusing fingers. Instead of being fishers of
the lost, we become critics of the saved. Rather than
helping the hurting, we hurt the helpers.[2]

We believe that the real enemy is not Christians from different franchises but Satan. Satan is wreaking havoc in our
world. He exploits addictive personalities with drugs, money,
and sex. He hurts children by destroying the marriage of their
parents. He abuses children by means of media that convince
them that sex is entertainment without undesirable conse-
quences. He so completely hardens the hearts of some people that they lie, steal, and murder without conscience. They
kidnap, rape, and murder little children. They bomb federal
buildings in Oklahoma and smash jets into the World Trade
Center and Pentagon. They oppress women, corrupt men,
and take advantage of children. People who do these things
are enemies of righteousness because they have been enslaved by His Satanic Majesty.

Our task in the world is to protect people from his evil intentions by modeling a better way. It is to comfort and salvage people who have already been made his victims and to try to give them hope for something positive. It is to liberate those who have been enslaved to drugs and sex, money and power. It is to push back the lies of Satan first by living and then by declaring the truth of Jesus Christ.

Don't let anyone hear what we have said here as a sort of New Age Relativism that says, "Oh, everybody's okay. It doesn't matter what people believe, just so they believe something!" We affirm that Christianity is the one true religion approved of God. We believe the exclusive claim made by our Lord Jesus Christ: "I am the way, and the truth, and the life. No one comes to the Father except through me" (John 14:6). But the best apologetic we have for convincing people that Jesus is their hope for eternal life is less through logical fisticuffs than the demonstration of mercy, kindness, joy, and love—the very things that Jesus used to draw people to himself. Yes, there are good rational arguments for the Christian faith. But those arguments fall flat when made by brassy, rude, and condescending people who come across as small-minded and self-righteous.

One writer who has addressed this issue of Christian distinctiveness within a pluralistic and relativistic world makes these three suggestions:

> First, the church must present the Christian faith not as one religious army at war against all other religious armies but as one of many religious armies fighting against evil, falsehood, destruction, darkness, and injustice. It respects and values its colleagues in the

fight; without their restraining influence on the darker aspects of human nature, this world would be in much more trouble than it is. *[Note: In the post-9/11 world, Christians, Muslims, Jews, and all other persons of goodwill must somehow learn to link arms against fanatics. The rules have changed in a world that has evil people training and arming terrorists. It would be irresponsible and unchristian not to applaud the Muslim cleric or atheist who uses personal and political influence to restrain murder and mayhem.]* This is an important distinction and reflects an important shift in tone and strategy. But to stop here would be a partial surrender to relativism.

The second thing, then, is that the church must call people to join an army, to sign up in the fight against evil—and not only evil out there but also evil in here, in our own hearts and in our own religions. The church must call people from being part of the problem to becoming part of the solution. But the task is not yet finished. Which army will people join? In a pluralistic world, there are many choices.

So, third, the church must help people decide which army to join. Contrary to relativism's implications, it does matter which army one joins. Why join the Christian cause? Why not another? Here is where the new apologetic gets put to work.

If people decide to "suit up" in the Christian cause, the church will have to help them get through spiritual boot camp. But by then, we have moved beyond apologetics and into program.

People are sick of religious fighting with each other (except, of course, some of those doing the fighting!). Most of us don't want to embrace another religion that is peddled by so many cranky people.

However, the religion that can enlist people in a fight with evil—wherever it is found, including in our own hearts and religious communities and systems—that religion will win their hearts. The religion that sees the pride in Pharisees "in here" and the devotion in prostitutes "out there," the religion that hears Satan whispering in the top disciple and that sees love exemplified in a Samaritan wayfarer—that religion will inspire their allegiance. The religion that recognizes its worthlessness if it's all talk and no action (all leaves and no fruit)—that religion will get them out of bed on Sunday morning, and more. The religion that sees true faith wherever it is found—including in an "outsider" from the "wrong" background, such as a Roman centurion or a Syrophoenician woman (see Luke 7:1-10 and Mark 7:24-30)—and not only sees it, but also affirms it, accepts it, commends it, celebrates it—that religion will win them for life. But wait! Aren't we talking about the kingdom of God, proclaimed and demonstrated by Jesus Christ?[3]

Indeed, that *is* what we're talking about. But the sectarianism of the modern world has all but blinded us to the kingdom-vision of Jesus. We have split so many theological hairs that we have forgotten the words of the apostle: "The kingdom of God is not food and drink but righteousness and peace and joy in the Holy Spirit" (Rom.14:18). The church of God at Rome was being diverted from its mission of being a second incarnation of Jesus to that city by having its members embroiled in judging one another over acceptable and unacceptable food, suitable and unsuitable drink. Before we laugh and feel too smug, those same debates still rage among Christians. Add to those issues the later accumulation of eschatologies, pneumatologies, ecclesiologies, "worship wars," and a host of other topics—none of which the Christians you read about on the pages of the New Testament had ever heard of and on which they had taken no "position"—and you realize the mocking laughter may be more appropriate to our situation than theirs.

> *The church has often been more concerned to prove itself right than to present the message which by its transforming effect is its own proof.*
>
> –Myron S. Augsburger

We believe too—and with strong emphasis—that the insights proposed, suggestions offered, and questions raised in this book are anything but definitive. Christian leaders must be "light on our feet" in these times, for our world situation no longer changes by century, generation, or decade. It can now be altered in a few days—perhaps even in a matter of hours. And while we believe the major paradigm shift from modernity to postmodernity is one with significance for the foreseeable future, it will not last for long. What will replace it is unknown to anyone—but God.

Conclusion

What we believe to be the single certainty amidst the uncertainty all of us acknowledge is Jesus Christ. With the author of Hebrews, we believe that "Jesus Christ is the same yesterday and today and forever" (Heb.13:8). Not the church. Not theology. Not cultural paradigms. But Jesus. *Jesus!*

Our personal security will be found in seeking him humbly and with hearts that are teachable. A faith community that affirms and supports that search is invaluable to its success for any among us. The hallmark of life within such a community will be visible love (i.e., care, regard) not only for its own but for strangers also. The fruit produced by these healthy churches will be redemption in Christ—redeemed lives, redeemed families, redeemed communities. The good works, love, unselfish spirit, joy, gentleness, and authentic trust in God lived by such a community—in partnership and affirmation with its sister societies of believers in Christ—combine to make its existence an appealing presence whose very life is an invitation drawing others to Jesus.

Notes

1. http://www.cnn.com/2002/US/07/28/mine.conditions/index.html.
2. Max Lucado, *In the Eye of the Storm* (Dallas: Word, 1991), pp. 56-57.
3. Brian D. McLaren, *Reinventing Your Church* (Grand Rapids: Zondervan, 1998), pp. 83-84.